LIFE
love
LEMONADE

stories of healing
and
overcoming life's lemons

LIFE love LEMONADE

stories of healing and overcoming life's lemons

TANIA JANE MORAES-VAZ
ANDREA MOURAD, ANDREA SLUGA, ANITA VOLIKIS
ERIN MONTGOMERY, TRACY LYNNE KEEPING, MICHELLE NICOLET
JENNIFER O'HARE, KIRSTI STUBBS COLEMAN, KAT INOKAI
TONI RONAYNE, MICHELLE TONN, MELISSA PUNAMBOLAM
GINA BRIGANDI, CASIE SCOREY, NATHALIE AMLANI
CHIARA FRITZLER, STEPHANIE DINSMORE, JULIE CASS

Published in Canada, for Global Distribution

by YGTMedia Co.

www.ygtmama.com/publishing

To order additional copies of this book:

publishing@ygtmama.com

Developmental Editing by Tania Jane Moraes-Vaz

Edited by Christine Stock

Book design by Doris Chung

Cover design by Michelle Fairbanks

ePub & Kindle editions by Ellie Silpa

Printed in North America

table of contents

introduction

The year was 2020. It was a year where I, like many, looked forward to all the things it held . . . all the dreams I would birth in it . . . all the promises I would go on to keep—to my family, and most of all, to myself. It was a year where I had prayed and asked God for expanse, strength, and community (and *expansiveness* was my word of the year). Oh, and traveling to and speaking at various retreats also made the top of my vision board. You bet your sweet soul I entered the year with guns blazing and with massive FU energy because sometimes, that is all the fuel you need to get out of your own way.

And get out of my own way I did. The year started off with some incredible events I had the fortune of attending. And in March, I hosted my first live event where I got to hug my fellow women in business, share stories of growth and healing, and have a mini vendor market. But little did I know that YGTM's Boss Mama Retreat would be the last in-person event I'd attend before the year took a turn for the uncertain and forced many of us to pivot, adapt, and evolve hard and fast.

And the precursors of that started with the tragic death of Kobe Bryant and his daughter. Still, the year continued on. The Super Bowl performances by JLo and Shakira were the talk of the town, and everyone and their grandma had an opinion about them. Looking back now, wow, talk about #firstworldproblems. If only I knew then what I know now . . . which is why it is said that life is lived prospectively but only understood retrospectively.

I remember the moment clearly—the moment when life as we knew it came to a complete standstill. The date was March 12, 2020, and the clock read 3:02 p.m. when I first heard news about the nationwide lockdown on the television at my client's house. You see, there had been whispers of a full-blown global pandemic for the first two months of the year, but life had continued as usual until this moment. I can still smell the aroma of warm brie and smoked meat and feel the palpable energy in the room—excitement, connection, and ambition accompanied with an underlying current of panic and uncertainty. I went on clicking away (I was there for a photoshoot), sipping on my mocktail and taking in the collective energy. Everyone put on a smile and slowly addressed the elephant in the room: businesses would be shut down for two weeks and March break would be extended. We felt hopeful. Okay, yes, a break would be kinda nice . . . to not have to rush . . . to have the kids home . . . to actually have a reason to slow down and be intentional. At least those were my thoughts at the time, which, in hindsight, is quite eye-opening and sad that we need a reason to slow down instead of consciously choosing to live with intention, consciously choosing to pause in every moment of our day.

It was in the early days of the first lockdown that the YGTM team conceived the idea of this anthology. It was born from the burning desire of a group of twenty mamas who got together in a mastermind in an effort to stay connected and keep the growth mindset going in life and business (Lord knows they needed it now more than ever).

Two weeks soon extended to two months, then six months, and now here we are—a whole year later. Evolved. Online events and summits are glamorous affairs complete with gourmet VIP swag boxes. Work, personal life, and business and corporate careers are all enmeshed in a smorgasbord of children poking and prodding for attention and assistance every few minutes. People attend Zoom meetings looking "business chic" on top and "I woke up in my pjs" on the bottom. Parents have taken on more capes than ever before, including the permanent role of designated snack bitch, tech support, playmate and entertainer, and much more. Children have gone from eager beavers with little curious minds to wondering why they are no longer allowed to hug their friends or see their teachers in person. Rites of passage such as graduation and prom, school dances, first kisses, playdates, and sleepovers are all gone—at least for the generation that lived in 2020.

The year 2020 was also the year of *la revolution*, on every front. It forced us to own our ignorance and brought us to our knees in acknowledgment of all our sociocultural biases and prejudices. It compelled us to have the uncomfortable conversations, to do the emotional work, to raise our consciousness on the experiences of BIPOC individuals and those living with disability, to lean into our free thinking, and to respect many differing perspectives. It was the year that has proven that posting a picture on social media doesn't mean your part in the community is done. In fact, the work is far from done. It has shown us that our activism lies not in posting pretty graphics and stories but having the audacity to be vocal and share our experiences, share our truth, and hold space for one another. Our activism lies in amplifying diverse voices and experiences. Our activism lies in our ethos of who we are, what our vision is, and that for which we stand.

Let's face it, 2020. You were incredible in many ways: for me and my business, for my personal growth, and for my relationships. But in so many other ways, you were harsh, triggering, and overwhelming. And growth often feels exactly like that—like you are living in survival mode. In fact, it still feels this way. It is as if we are reliving an incredibly weird sci-fi movie replaying the same loop over and over again. Open today, locked down tomorrow. It's like that relationship you know you need to end but for some reason you keep going back. Actually, it's like you keep getting sucked back in. Yes, 2020, you are that familiar frenemy. Want to know something, though? It was also the year that we each chose to become the star of our own movie. We made lemonade, margaritas, kombucha, all our fav drinks . . . we went ahead and made it happen, as best as we could, for us and our families, for our businesses, for our clients. We survived. The year 2020 is the year we chose to make lemonade from every type of lemon: battered, bruised, or even perfectly ripened yellow. The year 2020 is when we chose to appreciate the cards we are dealt and to rise from the depths of rock bottom, in some cases. And in many ways, we learned to shift into who we are.

Many of us, myself included, went full throttle into our businesses. Some of us found more aligned jobs, birthed business babies, and housed a beautiful little life within us that will have arrived earth side by the time this book is published. And some of us chose to honor the grief and sit with it. Some of us ended relationships and partnerships, while others found a new love so true. And many of us deepened the love we share with ourselves. We reparented and nourished ourselves (I swear, if we were playing the game Never Have I Ever, I'd be drunk very soon for all the days I've indulged in my self-care rituals, many of which include shopping online from my fav boutiques in an attempt to do my part and support small businesses). We honored our boundaries, stated our truth, and lived in alignment with that truth. We released anything that no longer fits who we are or where we are going. Every single act has been a feat of mighty love and courage wrapped in a bow of fierceness and vulnerability. One thing is certain, however. This past year was whatever we chose to make of it. We defied the statistics and persevered against all odds. We were warrior women who stood in our truth and spoke it boldly, freely, and unapologetically while honoring our season of awakening, reckoning, and becoming.

As you read through each word of these chapters, know that every single one of these women have come face-to-face with their demons. They have battled them, slain them, and have risen up every single time, no matter what that looked like. This book is filled with powerful, vulnerable, and bone-chilling truths that will bring you to tears and unravel your tightly wound self a bit more until you feel weightless and free, bold, courageous, and expansive enough to be who you are and who you are meant to be.

An ode to YOU, dear Warrior Womxn.

You deserve to be heard.
You deserve to be seen.
Your heart, your worth, your soul.
All precious gems well worth your very best effort, your finest shot.

You deserve to give yourself, your best self. And others too.

You deserve to live a life that makes you feel like a thousand Romanov candles lighting up the sky.

You deserve to be loved, cherished, and appreciated.

You deserve to be your own best friend first.

You, my dear, have been sprinting this marathon for ages.

Slow your stride if you must, but don't you dare give up.

Remember, there is pleasure in the pause . . . and treasure in the loss.

You, my dear, have been all things to all people your whole life.

Turn inward for a change. Mine the gems that lie within your heart and soul.

Trust yourself. Trust your intuition. Hear her call. You know more than you think.

You, my dear, have been graced with wisdom beyond your years.

You, my dear, have borne the pain of several generations and paid the price of several lifetimes.

You, my dear, have been guided to this exact moment by Divinity.

You have been training for this your whole life, even if it doesn't feel like it.

Trust yourself more. Jump.

Leap. Fly. Soar. Be seen. Be heard.

You've got this. Now go show 'em what you're made of.

~ Tania Jane Moraes-Vaz Editor in Chief, YGTMama Inc.

chapter 1

REPARENTING MYSELF TO BECOME ME

ANDREA MOURAD

"I needed to mother myself. I needed to reparent myself, the same way I was parenting my son—with love, confidence, faith, and nourishment."

IG: @ANDREAMOURAD01
FB: ANDREA MOURAD

ANDREA MOURAD

Andrea Mourad is a compassionate and devoted wife, mother, elementary school teacher, and writer. She has a master's degree in education and a bachelor's degree in psychology. It was through her recovery journey from chronic illness and two devastating miscarriages some years later that she discovered that although she loves her roles as wife, mother, daughter, and teacher, there was so much more to her that had yet to be explored. From there, her self-discovery journey began. During this time, she developed a newfound passion for writing and all things health, healing, and holistic wellness. Her unwavering strength and her will to celebrate life, even through the most challenging of times, have been her most praised assets. She believes that absolutely anything in life that is desired is achievable with the right mindset, the right plan of action, and the unshakable will to succeed. In her spare time, Andrea enjoys hiking with her family, rock climbing, skiing, yoga, and reading. She lives in Toronto with her husband and their vibrantly curious little boy, Marcus.

For my son, Marcus. You are my dream come true.

"Even after all this time, the Sun never says to the Earth, 'You owe me.' Look what happens to a love like that. It lights the whole sky."

~ Hafiz

A mother's love is like the sun. It gives and gives without expectation of anything in return. All the sun wants is to see Earth shine and flourish. The sun rises each morning, without fail, to ensure Earth receives its required and desired nourishment. A mother, to me, is the same. She is consistent and nourishing and has the potential to provide light and warmth to an entire community. A mother's love is the food and water that feeds our soul in the most magnificent of ways. A mother is sustenance on the brightest and darkest of days.

When I was a little girl, I always dreamed of becoming a mother and having a happy, loving home. It would be a safe, playful space for my kids to feel nourished, grow, and thrive. It would be a place where my husband and I openly and freely expressed our love and admiration for one another. A home where our kids could bring their friends over and feel proud of who they were and where they came from. It would be perfect. I would make sure it was! Every chance I had, I would use my dolls and my imagination to create this perfect little family I envisioned for myself. I dreamed up every aspect of this life I would have—my home and how beautifully furnished and well-kept it would be, my four beautiful, smart, and healthy children, my career/passion project that would give me life each day, and my tall, handsome, smart, athletic, lovingly wonderful husband. We would travel the world together and immerse ourselves in the magical beauty of various cultures, communities, and experiences. We would indulge in cuisine from around the globe, engulf ourselves in the unending beauty of Mother Nature, and explore this planet with curiosity, love, and kindness. Our home would always be full of life, adventure, love, family, and activity. This dream wrapped me up like a warm hug and made me feel safe, content, and at peace. This dream gave me immense joy and hope that my future was bright and there was so much to look forward to. This dream was my best kept secret that I could take with me wherever I went, regardless of how light or dark the places I would go could be.

As a child, you see, I grew up in a home with a tremendous amount of love but also a great deal of struggle and fighting between my parents. My father is a refugee, and my mother was raised by immigrants. They are of different religions but similar cultural backgrounds. My mother suffered most of her life with clinical depression, something that wore her out and significantly dimmed her light. We all carried this constant unending pain with her, but in our own, quiet ways. Pride was a big word in our culture and was a heavy bag to carry. I came from a Lebanese and Palestinian background. Honor and familial pride were cornerstones of our culture, especially for a girl. A family in turmoil was not a respectable family and was certainly not one "good families" wanted to be associated with. We were already different because my parents were of different faiths, so it was important for us to keep it together to prove that our differences were not problematic. The funny part was that faith and religion were never the issue in my home. To my parents and me, Christianity and Islam were very similar. They had some foundational differences, of course, but we never focused on those differences, so they were never an issue. For years and years, my family kept our problems a secret and my mother continued to suffer in silence with her depression. Since counseling was not well received back then and never seemed to help my mom, I spent a good part of my childhood trying to resolve my mother's inner struggles and my parents' marital hardships. I wore many hats as a child, but the hardest one to wear was being an only child. It was lonely in my house with all the arguments and negativity. I grew up with a lot of sadness and pain as a result of my parents' conflicts and my mother's mental health. I so badly wanted to belong somewhere. I wanted a community that knew me, all of me, and loved me anyway. Often, when my parents would argue, I would stand in between them, hoping that they would see me or hear me and realize that whatever they were arguing about was not worth it. That because of me, they would make it work, and our home would be that cozy and warm place I often dreamed it could be. I spent many mornings and evenings curled up in a fetal position in my bed with my door closed and my stomach in knots, listening to their fights and praying that they would stop. It was the beginning of my gut health issues and my feelings of uncertainty, instability, and immense insecurity in myself and in the foundational fabric that began to make up who I was. All I ever wished for was a happy, loving, "normal" home that I could feel safe in and call my own—a home that I was proud to belong to and show off to the world. Unfortunately, this wish for my first family was never realized since my parents decided to separate and then eventually divorce during my teenage years. Although it was an amicable divorce and they remain friends to this day, I still remember everything about the day my father left home. It was the most heartbreaking, soul-crushing day of my life. I can still see the pain in my father's face as he walked out our front door after saying his good-byes to me. I was and will always be my daddy's little girl. Allow me to explain . . .

When I was two, it was discovered that I had profound hearing loss in my right ear. The doctors believed that I'd likely lose my hearing altogether before adulthood, so they encouraged my parents *not* to speak to me in Arabic, their first language. Although well-intentioned, my parents had radically different views on the prognosis of my future hearing loss and responded very differently as a result. My mother went out of her way to ensure I had all the extra support I might need at school and wherever else I went. She used the disability card a lot. In hindsight, I know she was only doing what she knew at the time and what she felt was best. However, I hated every bit of it! It made me feel small. I didn't want to be singled out because of my hearing loss. I didn't want my teachers to start every school year with my new class, informing my peers that I was deaf in one ear. I did not want the teachers to ask my classmates to take pity on me in the school yard if they found me alone. Every year that this class conversation took place, I shrank a little more. My insecurities heightened and my world further crumbled. My father stayed quiet for a while and let my mother do what she felt was best.

One Sunday, when my dad and I were on our usual Sunday morning bike ride, he pulled over and asked me to sit beside him on the curb. He spoke to me in a voice he rarely used with me. I was listening. He told me not to pay too much attention to what the doctors said and to live my life without fear. He said that I could be whoever I wanted to be and do whatever I desired as long as I wholeheartedly believed in myself. All I needed was unwavering faith in myself and my dreams. He told me to be firm with anyone who tried to tell me otherwise. I don't know why, but I believed him. I still remember my eyes growing wide as he spoke, as large windows of possibility and hope began to open up for me like a warm summer breeze. I felt free like a bird let out of a cage, able to spread her big, beautiful wings for the first time. I was no longer defined by my labels. My life was up to me. My dreams were possible. What a feeling! I remember smiling the biggest smile I could. With warm, fresh tears running down my cheeks, I jumped into my father's arms. He probably doesn't know it, but he gave me a gift that day. He gave me back my power.

From that day, my life changed. Every time my insecurities started creeping up, my father's voice would pop into my head to remind me that I was unstoppable, capable, and worthy of my desires, so long as I devoted myself to my dreams. I lived the latter part of my childhood, teenage years, and adult life proving people wrong. I could hear as much as I needed to hear, and I didn't want any special treatment or unnecessary favors. I was a young girl filled with a lot of passion and excitement for life. I was a dancing queen, a free spirit, someone who always went out of her way to live out loud and in color. Anytime I was made to feel small, or like I belonged in a box, I allowed the words my father spoke to nourish me, strengthen me, and guide me as I continued in my lane.

When I was thirty, I met my husband. He was my unexpected Prince Charming that I dreamed of as a kid. We traveled together, we dreamed together, we walked many miles together. He made me feel as if we could achieve anything in life if we had the right intentions and dedicated the right time and effort toward it. He lived his life this way, and I loved watching the intensity in his eyes light up when he shared his big ideas with me. He proposed to me in Central Park, New York City, eight months after we met, and that was probably one of the happiest days of my life. We decided to start trying for our first baby about six months after we got married. I wasn't entirely sure that I was ready, but I didn't put up much of a fuss. I never, ever in my wildest dreams imagined it would be hard. Neither of us did. We ended up at the fertility clinic after a year of trying. It was a stressful first month of cycle monitoring, but we were among the lucky ones. We got pregnant in the first cycle. We were on cloud nine for about two months. But around the eighth week, I became very ill. I ended up in the hospital where I took what felt like thousands of tests. It was discovered I had developed ulcerative colitis in my pregnancy. Though I was relieved because I had a proper diagnosis and I wasn't dying of cancer (one of my many fears), I was also so very heartbroken. In an effort to save my baby, I'd be on an overwhelming medical protocol for the remainder of my pregnancy, and likely beyond. I have never done well with medications. I am a health nut who actually enjoys eating salads and making smoothies. *So how was this happening to me? What did I do wrong?*

With my mind racing and my body weak, we came up with a plan of action. I carefully put together a team of naturopaths, acupuncturists, doctors, and nutritionists to support me. I listened to my intuition and followed the advice that was aligned with my belief in healing through food and mental wellness. I continued to take the medications prescribed by my doctors, as I wasn't willing to risk losing this baby, but I did it my way. We hired a chef who was trained to help people with my strict dietary requirements, and we had a revolving door of family members who came over to check on me until I was able to get back on my feet. I recovered relatively quickly considering how sick I was, and I ended up having the most beautiful pregnancy, labor, and delivery. At thirty-nine weeks, we had a perfect baby boy who simply took my breath away. Motherhood has truly been the most magical, vulnerable, extraordinary experience of my life. I had no idea what to expect. I had no idea how much I could love another being. I had no idea how much would change. And I had no idea that I would lose myself in the process.

Because I had a turbulent relationship with my mother and a difficult childhood, I vowed that when I had children, I would do everything in my power to ensure that they felt loved and cared for. I wanted them to feel totally fearless to be whoever they wanted to be. I wanted to be their comfort and security. From day one, I focused on and worked toward just that. I wanted to be that mother who had her shit together no matter what. I did it all. I made sure our home was kept clean and tidy. There was always a fridge full of beautifully prepared meals and healthy snacks. I took care of my physical appearance and worked hard not to fall apart in the postpartum phase. Looking good made me feel good and like I was still me but only better because I had my little guy in tow. Every moment was devoted to my son, my husband, and my household. Outside of caring for my appearance, I completely forgot about me. I started to miss the woman I once was. The one who enjoyed salsa dancing, volleyball, painting, bike riding, rock climbing, and more. I stopped doing it all. My focus was my family.

When my son was one year, my husband and I started trying for our second child. This attempt also proved to be a challenging process. With the help of my traditional Chinese medicine doctor (who is also trained in Western medicine), I was able to conceive naturally and in good health one year later. My colitis was completely under control without medications, and I felt fantastic. My dreams were coming to life. I was in a place of extreme gratitude, often giddy with excitement. But at my three-month ultrasound, no heartbeat was detected. My world collapsed. Our little, precious baby was no longer living. I was in shock. *How? Why? What did I do wrong? When did it happen? Why didn't I feel anything?* The pain, guilt, and extreme sadness flooded every pore of my being. It felt toxic and unending. I couldn't sleep. I didn't want to eat. I could hardly look at my son. I felt like I failed him by being unable to carry his sibling to life here with us. I felt like I was failing my dream of having a large family, the one I pictured as a little girl. Yet again, my husband was the one to pick me up off the floor and breathe life back into my lungs. He made me feel completely safe, loved, and that we would get through this tragedy stronger and better because of it. I didn't know how, but much like my father's words, I believed him. I so badly wanted to be okay. Then, only a few short months later, we had our second miscarriage. This time, I wasn't crushed. Instead, something within me shifted. I needed to change. The way I was living my life, my worldview, wasn't working anymore. That's when it hit me. I needed to mother myself. I needed to reparent myself the same way I was parenting my son—with love, confidence, faith, and nourishment. I was more than a mother and a wife. I was *me* first, before I became a wife and a mother. I wanted me back. *Where did I go? Who did I become? Why did I feel so inadequate? What did I love to do? What were my passions?* I had no idea how to answer any of these questions. I didn't know me anymore. *What happened to me?* This was the first day of my self-discovery journey. This was the first day I remembered *I* mattered, and I had immense value quite simply because I was me.

Determined to find that woman again, no longer letting her hide in the shadows of her identities, I released my need for perfection. Only I expected such unachievable perfection. It was time to release that pressure. It didn't feel good or aligned to completely give of myself at the detriment of my health and well-being, at the death of my passions, at the cost of my identity as a woman. Taking care of me, however, felt too luxurious and made me incredibly uncomfortable. Asking for help still felt irresponsible; I was guilt-ridden with feelings of failure and not being enough. As I moved through this healing, unlearning, and uncovering process, I became more sensitive to recognizing and feeling negative energy. Before, when something didn't feel right, I would push it away and it would *fade* into the background. Not anymore. I could no longer ignore these hunches. My mind and body wouldn't let me. Yet still, my voice was frozen. Communication was and still is so challenging for me. Something felt totally wrong, but I was paralyzed in fear. Since I was a little girl, I learned that communication led to arguments and turmoil, which ultimately led to a broken home. I learned that if you just let things go, there would be peace. I did not understand the enormous price of "keeping that peace." In all my relationships, romantic and otherwise, I stayed silent. I didn't want to rock the boat. I didn't want to hurt anyone. I needed to keep the *peace*. I did not feel I was worthy enough to be heard. I didn't feel I had anything important to say. After my second miscarriage, I finally asked the questions: *Why? Why was I allowing myself to be silenced? Why was I afraid to rock the boat? Why did I feel unworthy?* These tough questions led me to the realization that this silent woman is absolutely NOT the woman I wanted to be. I felt this huge nudge. I had an obligation to teach my son what a strong woman looked like. Keeping quiet is not a lesson that I want passed down from generation to generation. *Where is my voice? Why won't it show itself? How do I find the courage to use it without hurting my ever-so-sensitive stomach? How do I take action? Where do I start?* The whisper of my heart then replied, "Baby steps, Andrea.

Listen closely. Lean in. Lean in. Lean in." And I did.

If there is anything you take away from my journey, let it be this: Allow your dreams to evolve. Mine sure did. While I dreamed of being a mother and having a large, happy, healthy family, I realized in my journey that I was seeking *me* all along. I was seeking my voice, my strength, my light, which I had let dim over the years. The embers still burned, only now I learned to stoke them and fan the flames, even when it felt uncomfortable. Know that at all times, spending time in solitude is a need, not a luxury. Self-care means whatever you want it to mean. And many times, it means advocating for healthy boundaries in your relationships, with yourself, and with others. It means standing in your truth and being vulnerable enough to let people see you for who you are. It means allowing yourself to be seen, heard, and felt the way you desire to be. Be daring enough to leap out of the box that people and their preconceived notions want to place you in. You will get better at it the more you do it. Be who you needed when you were growing up. Reparent yourself, love yourself, and believe in yourself, just as you would with your child(ren), partner, or loved ones. You matter. You are worthy. You are enough. Make progress, not perfection, your daily goal. You are a beautifully imperfect masterpiece who is refining herself with each passing moment, unapologetically who she was intended to be all along. My heart is overflowing with gratitude for this journey of mine that has brought me on this path. I now know it is safe for my dreams and desires to evolve and take up space while still being a good mother. Most of all, I now understand that a mother's love can be warm, tender, nurturing, and all encompassing, but only once she has first taken complete care of herself.

chapter 2

JUMPING IN

ANDREA SLUGA

"Don't ever think it's too late to start something wonderful and become that person who exists within."

ANDREA SLUGA

Andrea Sluga is a former award-winning sales professional turned mom-of-three household CEO and wife to the man of her dreams. She's a gratitude-giver, a marathon-finisher, and a champion for children with special needs. After giving birth to a son with a rare syndrome and overcoming his early health struggles, Andrea became passionate about helping other families in need. To date, she's raised over $100,000 for Silver Creek Preschool, a nonprofit, therapy-based program for children with special needs. When not brainstorming new ways to give back or sneaking vegetables into the kids' smoothies, Andrea enjoys exercising, bingeing on Netflix, and accidentally falling asleep with her kids.

To my family, thank you for filling my bucket with an abundance of love and joy. The world is a better place with you in it.

"It is far better to be exhausted from success
than to be rested from failure."
~ Mary Kay Ash

If you told me five years ago that I'd be receiving a community recognition award for my volunteer efforts in helping others in need, I would have wondered, *How? Why?* Five years ago, I was wrapped up in my own world, moving into a new home with two young children and trying to climb the corporate ladder, so to speak. Layering in volunteer work on top of all that was already going on for me would have been impossible. There was no time for that.

If you also told me five years ago that I'd become a mother to a child with special needs who would inspire me to start an annual fundraiser to help other special needs families, I'd have trouble believing it. The me five years ago was living in a bubble that did not include experience with real hardships or struggles. I was happily appreciating the things I had but doing nothing more to help others who had less. I was, in fact, living a very ignorant life.

But as you might know, a lot can change in five years, and for me, it has.

In summer 2016, I became a mother for the third time—to a beautiful son born with special needs. We did not know before the birth that he would enter the world with challenges, and it took us the better part of a year to finally breathe again. Surgeries, hospital stays, sleepless nights and anxiety-filled days were just some of the curveballs we encountered. Through genetic testing in early 2017, we were able to confirm the health and development issues of my son were caused by a rare syndrome called Rubinstein-Taybi—a condition characterized by feeding and growth issues, facial dysmorphia, microcephaly, eye abnormalities, heart and kidney defects, moderate to severe intellectual disability, and global developmental delays, among a few other things. At the time of this diagnosis, Antonio was already eight months of age, and the news came as more of a relief than a burden. My husband and I have always been an unbelievable team, and Antonio's challenges only strengthened what already existed in our marriage.

While I would never wish this time in our life on anyone else, it taught me lessons about life I've never before had to face. It showed me the strength of my character, my emotional coping skills, and my ability to roll with the punches. It was also through this hard time that I realized a beautiful dream, a new mission in my life living through my son's issues to support and inspire families whose children have special needs. Help was there when I needed it most, and I felt help should be there when others need it most too.

The vision I brought to life was a "fun run" named the *Toni-yo-yo Run for Fun*. Toni-yo-yo was a nickname given to Antonio early on by his sisters that stuck. It was my hope that he would one day walk his own run . . . a skill the doctors weren't sure was in his cards to do. Through the event, I partnered with Silver Creek Preschool in Etobicoke, Ontario—a therapy program for children with special needs where my son had been attending—to raise money and awareness for the center.

In year one I set a goal to raise $5,200, the full cost of one year's tuition, in order to send a child free of charge for a full year. The fundraiser was met with great enthusiasm from the community—more than 250 participants attended, and we raised a total of $44,000. The following year we raised another $58,000 with close to 400 participants. In two short years, over $100,000 supported the tuition for two families, the transportation fees for another sixteen families, and purchased new sunshades and play equipment to enhance the center's outdoor play space.

This small idea that turned into something bigger was more than I could have hoped for, but it's proof that it really only takes just one person to believe in something and then start doing it. That one ordinary person without extraordinary circumstance can make a difference. She just had to start somewhere.

In truth, I could give you a-million-and-one reasons why I was too busy, why the timing wasn't right, and why I should have never embarked on what I did. Others have even told me not to get involved in other causes, to focus on my own family first, and to take a few years to let Antonio's issues settle. But if I took the advice of others, I'd never have known all the good that I could, and did, accomplish. If I'd listened to those opinions and not to my own gut, I would have held back and refrained, and what a tragedy that would have been. It's amazing to know I've made an impact on others in more ways than one, and that I've created a path for my own children to look up to and admire.

I liked the life I used to have, but I love the life I'm living now because it's a life rooted in purpose. It's a privilege to know firsthand the struggles of others and then have the ability to do something meaningful about it. It's a feeling I wish everyone could experience. We all know the saying that it's better to give than receive, but when you actually do it and ask for nothing in return, it's a real gift.

I recently received an award of recognition for the efforts I've put forward in the community, and I was touched by the acknowledgement. When I had to postpone the third annual race last year due to the COVID-19 pandemic, I knew I'd still find ways to give back, and I did. I became a published author in the fall and donated back to Silver Creek through personal sales of the book. On top of it all, my son had his best year in development yet. He took independent steps last summer and started officially walking on his own a few months after.

To say that the fundraiser and my son's progress haven't been trying would be a lie. But nothing that is ever worth having comes easy. While things were on the up for the fundraiser and my son over the years, my own health was not optimal, and I had a few setbacks. I fought a viral infection for three months, had a major surgery, then had a setback in recovery. And most recently, I injured my arm.

When I said a lot can change in five years, I meant just that. For better or for worse, there are things that inevitably happen that shape what we go on to do and become. What I couldn't fully appreciate before I started my philanthropic journey was the impact these changes would have on my life and, in return, the impact I'd start having on the lives of others.

From the personal growth and many lessons I've had over the last five years, I now know that life is never straight or perfect. But I do believe anyone can do what I did and find deeper meaning in the lives they are currently living. We are often quick to dismiss our wildest dreams because we think they seem too big or unattainable or that we need certain things to line up first before we can dive in. But what if

I were to tell you nothing is impossible, and in fact the possible starts with you? I'm here to share how I made my dream happen because I honestly feel if I could do it, anyone else can too.

It starts with believing in yourself.

I've always believed I'm capable of doing anything I put my mind to doing, and most especially when it involves things I am passionate about . . . like running.

In May 2017, we were on our first family-of-five staycation in Niagara Falls, Canada, and it felt great to be staying somewhere other than a hospital. The kids and I registered for a 1K fun run, and afterward, I was to compete in the 5K race that followed. I remember the incredible energy I had that day because I put all my worry and fear to the side. I was so proud to be at that event, knowing how much we'd gone through leading up to it as a family and how much effort it took to get us there. The morning of the race, I decided to dedicate my run to Antonio. I planned to run my heart out, and I did just that. I went too fast right out the gate, but somehow managed to keep going, a testament to the new courage and strength that had built up inside me while caring for Antonio throughout that year. I finished that race in first place (women) and third overall (men and women) but winning was more than the medal I received that day. I left the race with a renewed sense of purpose, accomplishment, and ability. This is how the *Toni-yo-yo Run for Fun* came to be. I had taken inspiration from that very day and experience. It was as if the Universe was calling on me to pay this amazing energy forward.

When Antonio was born, an aunt shared with me a mantra that stuck: "Don't ever let yourself believe 'Poor me . . . Why me?' Instead, you must think, 'Why not me? Who better than me to be this child's mother?'" In that same way, when I started playing around with the idea to host a race, I rightly thought, *Why not me? Who better than me to lead with such passion and purpose and conviction?* Beyond the cutesy nickname, I named the race after Antonio because he continues to persevere against the odds, which in turn continues to give me hope for him, for us, for others.

Your efforts, no matter how small or big, will make a difference not only to you but to others somehow, somewhere, someday. There's always value to be had in taking a new journey, and when you believe in yourself, anything is possible and can be achieved. It just takes time to build.

Things only become real with a plan.

Big ideas always need a plan of action to execute or achieve. When I decided to put my energy into the fundraiser, I knew two things: I would fundraise for Silver Creek, and I would have the goal of raising $5,200 to pay the tuition fee for a child for a full year. After gaining the support of Silver Creek, I began the process of getting the other details together. I would need a website, a race partner for online sign-ups, permits, event promotion, and so much more.

The list of tasks to do grew, but it never felt insurmountable because I was continually driven with purpose. Late nights and curveballs were managed with smiles because I was committed to doing whatever it took. No one ever reaches the top without starting from the bottom, and you cannot escape hard work. People will want to fool you into believing success is all glamour without having to get your hands dirty, but your success is a direct result of how much hard work you're putting in.

It took months before I finally had something tangible about the race that I could share with others. During that time there were a few people who were privy to my plans, people I trusted and who I could turn to when I needed championing or an extra boost or a little push to keep going. I wanted to be sure I had a solid plan in place before welcoming the feedback and opinions of others. The person whose buy-in I needed most was my husband's. I knew actualizing this dream would take a lot of my time and energy, and I wasn't willing to commit to it without his support. Thankfully, I had his blessing from the very beginning. My advice is that you form an inner circle for yourself when you start, including people you trust to encourage you along and hold you accountable in a loving way.

Ask and you shall receive.

I've considered myself tremendously lucky for all the help we've received over the years, both with the race and in life with Antonio. I've also been privileged to witness such extreme acts of kindness and generosity through planning this race. There are more big hearts out there than one may realize and plenty of wonderful strangers in the community who want to care with you.

After enlisting my sister-in-law to help set up a website and securing a race partnership with Running Room to handle online registrations, I was ready to officially launch. I'd handled most of the planning on my own, but I knew achieving true success could not be done alone. I'd need a team to build my dream. I needed people to believe in my mission. I needed to put it all out there, and I did. I sent family and friends an email that outlined the fundraiser and pointed them to the website. I started social media channels and asked those I knew to share, like, and support the platform.

Once others got wind of my big plans, I was able to recruit volunteers to help on race day and in our promotion campaign and media outreach. People were willing to give me their time, and I was grateful for all of it. My friend's father is a talented graphic artist, and he stepped forward to design my logo. A colleague of my mother's, who'd just left a full-time position to start her own business, designed all of my race flyers pro bono. We'd never even met.

My first sponsor was the president of the board for Silver Creek and whose son also has special needs. She felt my energy and wanted to help me succeed. Other donors came forward after, and each small victory was like winning the lottery over and over again. When I started out, I didn't have a permit, I didn't have a budget, and I didn't have a promise that people would attend. All I did have was a strong belief in myself to succeed.

You can't predict how these kinds of things will all come together, but they do somehow. It's hard to tell someone to trust in this fact when they're starting out, but keep the faith. It may take time, but as word spreads and people get behind your vision, things have a way of turning out just the way you need when you lead with the right intentions.

Asking for help is not a sign of weakness or incompetence. It's no fun reaching the top only to realize you have nobody with which to share an amazing view.

Don't overthink. Just do.

There's never a "right" time to start something new, so I like to encourage others to jump in and do it. You cannot get anywhere if you don't start somewhere, and you cannot build on something when you've yet to create anything. You are ultimately in control of what you want and dream in life but overthinking those things too often kills the desire to move forward.

People who want it all figured out before they ever start planning will never take the risk. Begin with a goal and a plan and take it from there. Hurdles and roadblocks will always be there to overcome, but that's just it—you can overcome them with strong will, intention, and purpose.

That first year of the race was amazing, but I was so mentally exhausted afterward that I *almost* didn't plan a year two. A few things happened shortly after the event that made me reconsider where I was putting my focus and energy, especially after hearing from one neurologist who told us Antonio was severely challenged and would never walk independently in life. It wasn't the best news to hear and only added to my feelings of burnout.

I also began to worry about repeating the success of year one in year two. I knew what it had taken to achieve what we did, and I wasn't sure I was prepared to take on another year, at least not on my own. But I listened to what others were saying, and I'm glad I did. They told me what a shame it would be to throw away all that had been built, that the race was an amazing event in the community, and that there was nothing else like it to bring people together the way the race had done. So I did what any leader does: I put my head down once again and got to work on year two. I also asked for more help and was pleasantly surprised when my "team" grew. Sometimes, you can't assume people know what you need to make things happen, so you have to speak up and be honest—with others and yourself.

If you tell yourself that failing is not an option, it never will be. Had I worried about the budget, the permit process, and the many other hurdles we faced, I would have never started any of it, let alone do it two years in a row. It's easier to write off doing those things we know will be difficult, and it's easier to quit than it is to keep going, but anything worth doing takes hard work and effort, sacrifice, and commitment. Don't let the power of the mind sabotage your deepest wants and wishes. Those who continue to wait for the *right* time may find it never comes. Starting somewhere is always better than being nowhere.

You hold the ultimate power.

Everyone dreams, but so few of us know what to do with these dreams or how to make them something more. I firmly believe we have these special moments all the time, but we are too consumed by other things to let ourselves take hold of what the world is trying to tell us. When you feel incredible energy or have an amazing idea, don't ignore it. Write it down. Consider what can be done, then figure out how you can do it or who you can call upon to help you do it.

The next time you're in doubt of your own wishes and dreams, remember my humble beginnings. Back then I was just a mother who wanted to help others, and nothing then looked remotely close to where I am now and what's been accomplished. I ended up doing and gaining more than I ever thought possible, and you can too because every day is a new day to start living out all those dreams, big or small.

If you find yourself getting stuck at the start, have faith that taking the first leap in is usually the hardest part. Once you're flying, you'll inevitably be further ahead than from where you started and on a great path because it's the one you've made for yourself.

My final wish for you is this: Never stop believing in your beautiful self. Don't ever think it's too late to start something wonderful and become that person who exists within. It takes just one soul to make a difference, so take that first step forward. I guarantee you will never regret embarking on a journey of doing good in this world for yourself and others.

chapter 3

THE POWER OF SURRENDER

ANITA VOLIKIS

"And with that incredible release came the very thing that I had wanted with every fiber of my being. Instead of coming to me as the product of struggle and pain, motherhood came to me with flow, joy, gratitude, and endless love."

ANITA VOLIKIS

Anita Volikis is dedicated to helping others navigate life transitions with resilience, align with their passions and purpose, and embrace their best lives. She is a master life coach, NLP (neuro-linguistic programming) practitioner, lawyer, and author. Before obtaining her coaching certification, Anita practiced family law in Toronto for nineteen years. Anita is certified in The Better Apart® Method for divorce professionals and is committed to transforming the narrative of separation and divorce to something positive and empowering. A prolific writer, Anita has authored and edited two legal publications and has contributed to *Thrive Global* and *Mama Brain Magazine*. She lives in Toronto with her husband and son and their golden retriever.

For James—my sun, moon, and stars.

"Tell me, what is it you plan to do with your
one wild and precious life?"

- Mary Oliver

I gave birth to my son, my only child, at age forty-two. I hadn't
envisioned becoming a mother in my forties. That wasn't *part of the
plan*. But then again, I never expected that I would struggle with infertility, miscarry twice, and navigate assisted reproduction and adoption
before conceiving naturally and giving birth. At forty-two. None of
these things were "part of the plan."

What was the "plan," you ask? It was simple! Go to university, obtain
an undergraduate degree and then a law degree, begin my career, meet
and marry my "soul mate," become a mother, and live happily ever after.
Really. In that exact order. I liked to have my ducks in a row before
taking action. I didn't like surprises. I planned and then executed. This
strategy worked for many things. But not for everything.

Was this faith that things would work out or simply naïveté? Perhaps
it was a little of both. I now understand that you can approach life
with as much determination as you want, but that does not guarantee
events will unfold according to plan. As I navigated my thirties and

forties, I came to understand that *"most of life will unfold in accordance with forces far outside your control, regardless of what your mind says about it."*[1] The sooner you understand this fact and come to accept it, the less disappointment you will experience and the more joyful your journey will be. Isn't that the point? Shouldn't we be living, breathing, and extracting as much growth and joy from the journey instead of focusing on our final destination? I am grateful that I developed the awareness that I was losing sight of the journey because I was blinded by the destination. This awareness came from several experiences and life lessons. Let me take you through them.

I was a high achiever before I even heard the term or knew what it meant. I believed that I had to excel at *everything*. I was the textbook definition of the type A personality. And no, this was not the product of parental influence or pressure. My parents were my biggest cheerleaders, discouraging this type of all-or-nothing mentality. The pressure that I was experiencing was all self-created. Thankfully, I still had a lot of growing up to do.

As a high school and university student, I was a planner. I had goals and needed the steps to get there. Once I had those figured out, it was all about staying on course and not veering off track. When I decided I wanted to become a lawyer (again, my decision alone), I came up with a plan to get there. I remember meeting with my high school guidance counselor (in grade nine or ten) and announcing that I knew what I wanted to be when I grew up. I wanted to be a lawyer and needed a plan to get there. I knew I needed good grades (preferably in the nineties), but what courses did I need to take in the balance of high school and university to increase my chances of getting accepted to law school? My guidance counselor nodded her head, smiled, praised me for my determination, then proceeded to explain, in a very gentle way, that although it was wonderful that I was dreaming about my future, I should keep an open mind as I was bound to change it a few times in the coming years.

During my undergraduate program, I was methodical about the courses I took and what I majored in. Don't get me wrong; I enjoyed my university experience, took fantastic courses with amazing professors, met wonderful friends, and excelled. But the choices I made at the time were all restricted by my plan. If it didn't fit the plan, it didn't belong in my life. My ultimate goal was to achieve the grades that would get me into law school. I knew it was competitive and that I needed to work harder than ever. Unfortunately, the excellent work ethic I had developed by that time came at the expense of continuing a pursuit of music (a constant in my life until then) because I deemed it to be a distraction from reaching my goals.

I met my future husband when I was in my first year of law school at the University of Toronto. I had decided that I needed to develop some independence and moved into a graduate residence for the first two years of my three-year program. I met Jeff through his sister who lived in my residence. Our paths were unlikely to cross otherwise, as Jeff was pursuing his master's in molecular genetics at that time. We became friends and love soon blossomed.

I began practicing law at a boutique family law firm in Toronto at age twenty-eight and became engaged to Jeff a short time later. We married when I was twenty-nine and he was thirty. As for the mother-hood piece, my husband and I made what we then believed was the responsible decision to postpone starting a family for a few years. We were very happy. We went out to dinner every Friday. We went to jazz clubs regularly. We enjoyed frequent vacations. We took regular stay-cations. Life was good. But it was "not a good time" to start a family.

I was a new lawyer working twelve-hour days and Jeff was completing a PhD of several years in a highly competitive field. Our focus was on ourselves.

At the time, our marriage was characterized by making responsible financial decisions, spending our time the way that we wanted, and pursuing our careers. We envisioned a life with children, but we held the belief that life had to unfold a certain way before introducing children into our family: We had to be established in our jobs, have a certain level of savings, and own our first home. Quite the to-do list, isn't it?

It's funny how life happens. As it turned out, when we decided that the time was right to have a child, it apparently wasn't. It is difficult to articulate the overwhelming anguish that enveloped me during this time. My daily life was focused on a painful void. "Why me?" or more accurately, "Why not me?" became my daily mantra. It is strange how when we want something badly enough, we cannot have it. And yet the things we don't necessarily seek or believe that we need somehow fall into our lives with ease.

It is amazing how trying to have a baby can drain the romance and spontaneity out of a relationship. Now, we loved each other and had a close marriage, but timing intimacy around my ovulation cycle was not our idea of romance and doing so for any length of time has a way of making you feel tired and dejected. Then add the almost endless reminders of my "failure" to conceive—there's nothing like that to make one feel inadequate as a woman.

Everywhere I looked I was reminded of my inadequacy: pregnant women walking down the street, pregnant women at the grocery store, pregnant lawyers at court, pregnant colleagues at the office, pregnant cousins, pregnant friends, baby shower invitations, baby showers at the office, women pushing strollers, colleagues with their infants in tow.

On the outside, I feigned happiness, offered hugs, smiles, and congratu-lations, but on the inside, I was falling apart and silently screaming.

We tried to conceive for two years before we saw a fertility specialist. Two years may not sound like a very long time, but when you are in your mid to late thirties, it's an eternity. Tests and laparoscopic surgery uncovered that I had mild endometriosis, a condition that I had until then assumed meant "heavy periods," which I had experienced for many years. I later learned that endometriosis is frequently misdiagnosed and left untreated, as its symptoms are typically misunderstood. We were told that my mild endometriosis coupled with my age (I was thirty-seven by then) would make becoming pregnant "challenging" at best. One of my tests revealed that at the time of testing, I had what seemed to be a blocked fallopian tube. It was likely that my endometriosis was causing scarring that contributed to the blockage, but it was not known with any certainty, even after my first laparoscopic surgery. After the first of such surgeries, the specialist recommended in vitro fertilization (IVF). We made the decision to proceed while we were still in the examination room. And so began three years of tests, procedures, surgeries, injec-tions, egg retrievals, embryo transfers, hope, heartache, loss, sadness, resentment, anger, despair, and exhaustion.

We commenced our IVF journey with tremendous faith. I was aware that the statistics of getting pregnant in this manner (at my age and with endometriosis potentially blocking one fallopian tube) were not encouraging, but we remained hopeful.

The actual IVF process did not scare or worry me. I did not really mind the injections, blood tests, ultrasounds, and invasive procedures. I took significant time away from my law practice to complete two of the four cycles. I made changes to my daily life, including incorporating acupuncture into my routine.

Our first IVF cycle resulted in pregnancy. Our joy was short lived, however, when I miscarried at nine weeks. None of the other three attempts resulted in pregnancy. Less than a month after our third cycle, my in-laws were tragically killed in a house fire. The next few months were about managing our grief, dealing with legal responsibilities, and most importantly, healing and helping my husband through the most painful event in his lifetime. We focused on our emotional and mental well-being. We tried to move forward as best as we could. But we still wanted to become parents.

My in-laws had adopted two children: my husband, and two years later, his sister (they are not related biologically). Both were adopted as infants, and both were told as children about their birth and adoption stories. Jeff and I had talked about whether adoption would be an option for our family when we were experiencing our struggles, and we had decided that if we could not have biological children, we would adopt a child.

We decided that we would pursue domestic adoption, meaning within Canada. We completed our home study, took the required course, prepared and worked with a social worker, and fulfilled all the other requirements. Then we waited. And waited.

During this time, we made the difficult decision to try to get pregnant through IVF one last time because we had a single frozen embryo. This decision was made from a different place, that of obligation. We did not feel good about allowing our embryo to remain in a laboratory indefinitely. But it was obviously not ideal to be going through an IVF cycle when we had previously thought we had moved away from having a child biologically and had embraced adoption. The death of my in-laws and the difficult months that followed also made this a less-than-ideal time to make a decision and proceed with something as involved as assisted reproduction. In hindsight, my heart was not entirely in it.

While I was being maneuvered by the nurse during that embryo transfer, I felt a subtle but concerning snap in my lower back. Instead of spending the rest of the day relaxing and remaining calm, I was a bundle of nerves. I did not like how I was feeling. I had been quite calm following the previous IVF embryo transfers. This time, the next day I was in terrible pain and had trouble walking. When I learned what I had already known deep inside me, namely, that I was not pregnant, I scheduled an appointment with my doctor who was quite shocked that I had waited that long to see her. An MRI revealed that I had herniated two discs in my lower spine. I spent the next year intermittently lying on the floor of my office while taking phone calls and dictating correspondence, stopping several times during my hour-long drive to work to get out of the car (when I was able to go to the office), and seeing a chiropractor initially several times a week and later weekly and biweekly.

I felt incredibly defeated. The heartache of the previous three years had caught up with me. I wasn't the only one. Jeff felt it too. People who have not shared this experience forget that it is not only women who suffer during this time. Their partners go through it as well and often don't share how painful it is for them. Thankfully, Jeff and I talked about our feelings together and what we were going through. And together, we made the decision to grow our family a different way. We are both dog lovers and had dogs growing up. It was time to share our family with one. So, we adopted a puppy. One August day, we welcomed a nine-week-old, beautiful golden retriever into our home, and he slowly began to change our lives. It's true. Dylan changed our lives. We showered him with love, and we lived each day with gratitude and joy. We were a family.

We updated our adoption profile, revised our letter (the story—a short hardcover book—we wrote about our journey and family) to include our pup. He was, after all, a member of our family. We remained hopeful that our story would resonate with someone and we would be united with our child.

For the first time in years, my daily thoughts were no longer consumed by the desire to become a mother, by the resentment that it wasn't happening for me, and by the fear that I would be childless forever. In short, I let it go. Was I abandoning the desire to become a mother? No. I was abandoning the struggle. I was letting go of the fear, the lack, the resentment, and the anger. I finally began to trust. I trusted that motherhood would happen if, when, and how it was meant to happen. I no longer began and ended each day thinking, *Why can't I have a baby?* I stopped feeling excruciating disappointment with the arrival of my period each month, and I began to rejoice in the pregnancy news and birth celebrations of those around me. My marriage became energized again after years of being almost entirely focused on the goal of having a baby. I loved my husband, our puppy, our family, and our life together.

I still struggled with my back issues, which made managing a busy litigation practice very challenging. But truth be told, it was more than my injured back that was causing a shift; I was exhausted after years of physical and emotional stress. Looking back, I really don't understand how I did it. I suppose it was strength. But strength or not, it was impossible to simply continue the status quo. I decided to take a six-month sabbatical to give myself time to heal physically and emotionally and to decide whether I wanted to return to my career or make a change.

Two days after starting my sabbatical, I learned I was pregnant. It was the first time we had conceived naturally. I was stunned. I remember taking a photo of the positive pregnancy test because I doubted my ability to communicate the result to my husband. The next few weeks were a dream-like trance of happiness, nerves, and fear. I had experienced one miscarriage before, and I was terrified it would happen again. It did. I miscarried at about eight weeks. The fact that it was my second pregnancy loss did not make the event easier to understand or accept. I grieved it just as I had grieved my first pregnancy years earlier.

I slowly resumed my routine and once again embraced the things that had given me joy that spring and summer. We left our pup in the care of my parents and traveled to San Francisco and Monterey, California, for a week in September, during which time we celebrated our twelfth wedding anniversary. We returned from the trip refreshed and happy. A few days later, and just two days before my scheduled return to my firm, I learned I was pregnant. We were shocked and also elated. Conceiving naturally twice in six months? Holy shit. It was a miracle. I returned to my law practice feeling overjoyed and renewed. I couldn't stop smiling, even during difficult meetings and court appearances. Although I was still somewhat nervous given my history, I was not living in fear. I was consumed with joy and gratitude. Our son was born the following spring.

As I held my child in my arms for the first time, the feelings I experienced were indescribable. What I wanted so badly to manifest in my life was finally here, all because I chose to stop responding to the Universe with resentment, urgency, fear, and despair. I chose to give myself grace, and to let it all go. I did. I let it all go, surrendered to a higher power, and felt freer and happier than I had in years. And with that incredible release came the very thing that I had wanted with every fiber of my being. Instead of coming to me as the product of struggle and pain, motherhood came to me with flow, joy, gratitude, and endless love.

I have learned a valuable lesson in the last several years. We cannot control everything. In fact, there is little that we can control. Events occur, sometimes painful and tragic ones, that are not within our power to create or curate. The Universe unfolds in strange and sometimes excruciatingly unfair ways. Does this mean that we are powerless, passive beings? Absolutely not. While we may not control everything that happens in our lives, we do have control over our response and how we move through these experiences. We do have power, and we do have choices. So, choose faith, choose surrender, choose to trust in aligned timing. Only when we surrender whole-heartedly and allow the Universe to work her magic in our life do our deepest desires have the space to manifest.

chapter 4

THE HARVEST WE ARE DEALT

ERIN MONTGOMERY

"I didn't choose to be a single mom, I didn't choose divorce and heartache, but those were the lemons I was handed, and it was up to me to show up for myself and my kids, and to do so powerfully."

ERIN MONTGOMERY

Erin Montgomery is a journalism graduate and book editor. She has held positions in PR, marketing, and communications for the past fifteen years and is the editor and founder of *Flourish Magazine*, a quarterly magazine written for moms by moms. Erin is a single mom to three children ages two to ten. She splits her time between dance competitions, basketball games, and ninja warrior practices. She is a lover of all desserts and is an avid traveler. In the last few years Erin has returned to her roots as a writer, and more recently has become a published author. Erin is currently working toward her editing certificate with Simon Fraser University. Aside from work, you can find Erin hiking the trails with her kids, playing with her new puppy, Lola, and rediscovering what it really means to be in love.

My chapter is solely dedicated to my children. Without them, I wouldn't have realized my own strength. I wouldn't have been able to move forward and build a life for us. My children taught me resilience, they gave me unconditional love, and they showed me just how strong I really am. Being their mother has been my greatest joy and my hardest journey. I am truly grateful for them and all that they bring into my life.

"There is a stubbornness about me that never can bear to be frightened at the will of others. My courage always rises at every attempt to intimidate me."

~ Jane Austen

When life hands you lemons, you are supposed to make lemonade—but what happens when the lemons you're handed are moldy and a little more than past their expiration date? How do you turn those less-than-ideal lemons into that oh-so-sweet lemonade?

You start over. You plant new seeds, water those seeds, and watch them grow.

That's exactly what I did.

* * *

When I was twenty-four years old, I got married. We were seven months pregnant with our daughter at the time, and we jumped right into a marriage we weren't ready for. We did what was expected of us. We bought a home. We welcomed our daughter, and we "played" house.

We were married for eight years. In those eight years, we welcomed two more children, both boys. We were so good at playing house that I started to believe we were a happy couple. When you have been playing a specific role for a long time, it slowly starts to become your identity, and you have a difficult time realizing what the truth actually is.

That's why I was completely shocked when he announced that he wanted to separate. He had fallen "in love" with someone else. I was blindsided. I had just given birth to our third child four months earlier, I was working ridiculous hours almost every day so he could take paternity leave, *and this was how he was repaying me?*

When you are faced with a conversation about separation or divorce, the number of feelings that run through your body are vast and intense. I left that conversation feeling completely worthless. In the days and weeks that followed, I experienced much self-hatred. I felt like there must be something wrong with me because clearly, I wasn't good enough. I had become a shell of a person. I had no self-worth, no self-love, and no self-confidence.

I was a "happy" mom during the day, but meanwhile, I'd cry into my six-month-old son's blanket at night. I was miserable. I didn't understand how I was supposed to carry on. How was I supposed to be the cheerful, fun-loving mom who always wanted to take her kids on an adventure when I felt like I was unworthy of happiness and love?

Here's what I quickly realized: I had to pick myself up and dry my own tears because no one else was going to do it for me. I had to be the happy, fun mom because no one else was going to play that role. I had to show my kids that everything was going to be okay because no one else was going to.

It is amazing how much strength you can muster up when you realize that your kids need you, they are counting on you, they are looking at you to show them what comes next. Feeling sorry for myself wasn't going to keep a roof over our heads. It wasn't going to ease my kids' pain, and it sure as hell wasn't going to help us move forward. But let me make something clear: You are absolutely 100 percent allowed to feel the loss of your relationship. You are allowed to cry and scream. You are allowed to feel sorry for yourself. No one can tell you how to heal yourself or how long it should take you to "get over it." But there comes a point in that grieving process when you need to make that decision to move forward—when you need to turn your lemons into lemonade.

* * *

Within two months of our separation conversation, he moved out, and I was left to fend for myself and my kids. I was trapped in a house I couldn't afford, and I had to resort to borrowing money from my mom every month just so I could keep a roof over the kids' heads. Meanwhile, my husband became a person I no longer recognized. He flaunted his new relationship on social media, took getaways, and seemed to forget that he had responsibilities back home.

That first year following our separation, I was drowning in bills. But I pushed forward. I worked longer hours, and I missed A LOT of the first year of my son's life, but I knew that in the end it would be worth it. I needed to give my kids everything they were missing.

We finally sold our marital home just over a year after our initial separation conversation. It was a super long process, but the kids and I were finally free of the enormous financial burdens we had been facing. We moved in with my mom, and we started over. Within four months,

I was able to secure us our own place, I got a full-time job with regular hours, and I was able to keep the kids at their school.

But now I face the struggle of single motherhood. I am a full-time single mom. My kids see their dad every other weekend, but everything else lands on me. If one of them is sick, I use a vacation day. If one of them has a dental appointment, I have to leave work early. I am the taxi driver, the cook, the housecleaner, the good cop, and the bad cop. I also need to be present ALL THE TIME. Being a single mom is like being switched on every day but never being switched off. And then, when your battery starts to run low, you find two minutes to hide and recharge before they realize you are missing.

As a single mom, I don't get to trade off with another parent. I don't get to share household responsibilities, and I don't get to share the never-ending loads of laundry. But that's okay. My kids and I have figured out a new normal. We all have responsibilities, and we all show up for one another at the end of the day.

I am now almost four years into my journey as a single mom, and I have learned more in these past four years than I did during my eight-year marriage. My kids have taught me resilience, they have shown me unconditional love, they have taught me how to open myself up again, and they continue to surprise me each day. My kids have adjusted well to having just Mom around every day, all day. They have faced their share of roadblocks and hiccups, they have cried, they have expressed anger, and they have even spoken with a counselor, when needed. But if I look back over the last four years, I can see that this little family of mine has become so much stronger and so much closer.

Now, I don't want you to feel sorry for me. This chapter isn't meant to cause you heartache. I didn't write these words because I needed or wanted pity. I wrote this chapter because somewhere out there is a single mom (maybe you even know her) who is struggling. There is a mom who has been or is in my shoes and is about to walk down the same path I did. I want you to share this story with her. Becoming a single mom is difficult. It is one of the hardest things I have ever been through. But it is also one of the most rewarding. As a single mom, I never miss any smiles or giggles. I get to wipe away every tear. I get to receive double the hugs and kisses. I get to play silly video games with my sons and watch my daughter dance. I get to be present for every life event. While it may be twice the work and twice as hard, it's also twice as rewarding and twice as sweet.

To all the single moms out there, I see you and I understand you, and I am so excited to tell you that it does get better. It may not seem like it, but in a year from now you will see just how far you have come.

I didn't choose to be a single mom. I didn't choose divorce and heartache, but those were the lemons I was handed, and it was up to me to show up for myself and my kids, and to do so powerfully. It may have taken us nearly four years, but I can proudly say that my kids and I have turned those moldy, expired lemons into some of the sweetest lemonade I have ever tasted.

chapter 5

WHEN LIFE KNOCKS YOU DOWN, YOU PUNCH BACK WITH GRATITUDE AND GRIT

TRACY LYNNE KEEPING

"Life gets to feel good, taste good, and look good, just the way you want it to."

TRACY LYNNE KEEPING

Tracy Lynne Keeping has seen her fair share of tough times but always tries to maintain a positive and upbeat attitude toward it all. Since becoming a single mom, she has felt the spectrum of emotions and has struggled to maintain that positive attitude she is known for. After hitting rock bottom, Tracy Lynne realized there had to be more to life. Tired of the constant feeling of overwhelm and that sense of never enough, she embarked on a self-discovery journey. Slowly, her positive, can-do attitude returned. Tracy Lynne realized that she can't possibly be the only mom who has felt this way, and *LightenYourMotherload*, her popular blog, was born.

Tracy Lynne's passion lies in helping other moms ditch the mom guilt, stop the overwhelm, and shift their mindset so they can stop living a mediocre life and start creating the dream life they crave for themselves and their family. When she's not dancing in her car, she's having spontaneous dance parties in her living room or digging in the sand with her son at the beach or at the bike park while enjoying playdates with friends.

I dedicate this chapter to anyone who has been knocked down but got back up and kicked some ass. I see you. I'm cheering you on from the sidelines.

"You are braver than you believe, stronger than you seem, and smarter than you think."

~Christopher Robin

You know the saying, "When life hands you lemons . . . make lemonade?" Seriously, is there anything more fucking clichéd?

Meh, probably not. But I can honestly say that in the last couple of years I have made some of the most kick-ass lemonade with all the challenges that have come my way.

My life is pretty good right now, but it hasn't always been that way. To find out how I made this sweet AF lemonade, however, we need to back up to the beginning.

I have not been so lucky in love. All my life I have seemed to attract men who were damaged in some fashion, which then led to some form of emotional abuse (although I didn't recognize it at the time). It got to the point that I thought I was destined to be single forever because it felt easier to be alone than to deal with yet another asshole. What I didn't know then was that the reason I was attracting these types of men was due to an inside job. But I digress.

I didn't realize it at the time, but I know now in hindsight that we hold the key to creating our own delicious lemonade that will quench our thirst for whatever it is we need in each moment. Life gets to feel good, taste good, and look good, just the way you want it to. You may not nail the recipe on the first try, or even the second, but therein lies the joy of making your own lemonade. How did I create my own recipe? Well, I realized I needed . . .

A Dash of Courage

I had a good job, and I'd just bought my first condo in a very desirable Canadian city. Really, the only thing missing in my life was a relationship (even though I had told myself I was going to be very contentedly single forever). The Olympics were in town the winter after I bought my condo, and it was quite the party. But I wandered the streets alone for the most part, and it got me wondering why the heck I cared to stay in this town so much. Maybe it would be better to rent out or sell my condo and move on. I'd been in that town for about a decade, and with a failed marriage under my belt and no real friends to speak of, what was the fucking point? Maybe it was time to start fresh.

Just as I was looking into the possibility of moving across the country, what it would entail, and how I would go about finding a job, a man from my past showed up and basically swept me off my feet. I was "love-bombed," I believe the term is.

He came with a ready-made family, which suited me fine as I was on the fence about being a mom anyway and getting pregnant at thirty-nine seemed ludicrous. The only issue was that he lived in my old hometown and I lived on the mainland. However, after about a year of dating and on my fortieth birthday, he held a surprise party for me and proposed. I guess that sealed the deal! I was moving back to the island.

What I didn't know was what was in store for me once I moved back.

Things took a turn when I moved in with him, but I wasn't entirely sure what was happening. The sweet "love-bombing" guy was gone. *Where did he go?* Now, if I'm totally honest here, the change actually started while I was still on the mainland, but I ignored it. ALL the red flags were there, waving madly in the air, but I ignored every one of them. I kept telling myself that things would settle down once I moved in with him. Isn't that what every woman "in love" says? I wasn't listening to my gut. Time (and many bad decisions) had dulled my intuitive senses, which made it hard to trust those little nudges that you get when things aren't going right. Our relationship was not progressing the way I had pictured it in my head. Being forced into motherhood regardless of how I or the kids felt was wrong in my mind. There was constant pushing for his kids to call me "Mom" and constant badgering over housekeeping and how horrible I was at it (I mean, come on, he had seen how I kept my condo. Did he really think my cleaning habits were going to magically change once I moved in with him and his kids?). There were constant put-downs. But these things occurred so gradually, and done under what some might consider love, that I didn't even recognize it for the emotional abuse it was.

Then, the real kicker!

I became pregnant. At forty, no less. What the fuck was I thinking?

I had already been questioning the relationship before this news. Now? I hoped and prayed that things would improve with the pregnancy. The reality? Things escalated, and I started looking for ways out of the relationship. Could I afford to live on my own? Did I want to live on my own again? With a baby? I had no answers. All I knew was I wanted out, and I have to admit that I considered abortion because it felt like the only way I could be free of this situation I had gotten myself into. However, if that had happened, I would be writing a very different story.

Things kept escalating and came to a head for me after the little one was born. Our son was a couple of months old, and I decided to treat myself to a haircut and color, as I hadn't wanted to color my hair while I was pregnant. I came out of the appointment feeling pretty damn good about myself and loving my new look. Then he called via FaceTime (he was working out of town), and I happily showed off my new 'do. I don't recall much about the conversation other than that he said some incredibly cruel things. That was the beginning of the end for me.

Here is where the lemons start turning into lemonade.

A Pinch of Sass

At that point, I threatened to leave him but then didn't really do much about it. I did start packing a few boxes, but I was hoping the whole time he would smarten up. He didn't. We tried counseling, but all he did was blame me for everything and tell the counselor all the things he felt were wrong with me. Once I realized counseling wasn't going to work, I made a beeline for a lawyer with my questions. What would custody look like? What would visitation look like? Could he really get 50 percent custody? It took me a couple of months, but I finally got my stuff organized and left with a five-month-old in tow. It hit him out of left field. He really had thought I was going to stay.

I was a complete and utter hot mess for the first year and a half after leaving. I mean, I was barely functioning. I would shake and break out into a cold sweat any time I had to talk to him or about him with people I lovingly called the PTB (the Powers That Be for you *Buffy* fans). I had butterflies in my stomach, and I felt nauseated. You name it, I felt it. I could barely string a coherent thought together if it involved him. The only thing keeping me going was my child.

By year two I realized I could not keep functioning this way. I knew I was meant for more, that there was more to life than just the shell of a life I was living, and that was when I discovered life coaching. It opened a huge world for me and how I approached things. Within a short period of time I got to work on my mindset, and I realized just how much my inner dialogue was affecting my outer world. I was amazed by how even just a little shift in narrative like "I can't" to "I can" could change my outlook. I realized that my constant need to try and prove my side of things was feeding my anxiety and depression. This need kept me stuck in a dark spiral of *what ifs* and *how comes* and in that black hole in the pit of my stomach. As soon as I started to let go, I felt calmer, and the anxiety started to fade. The *what ifs* became less frequent, and the spiral of negative thoughts nearly disappeared, and if they happened, I began seeing them for what they were and could snap myself out of it within a relatively shorter period of time. What I would once fixate on for days became hours, then minutes. I realized that I was responsible for my own thoughts and emotions and thus, all the stress melted away.

Now?

I can laugh at the ridiculousness of it all.

I can see how I was the creator of all my negative feelings and how just some small shifts have completely changed the landscape of my life. I am on an upward trajectory that is so completely different than anything I could have imagined two or three years ago. I can so clearly see the victimhood mentality I was living in. I have clarity. I know what I'm here to do.

I have created a life I love. I have become a person I love. I am content. Happy, even! While I may not be exactly where I would like to be, doing exactly what I want to be doing, I know it will come. I trust the Universe implicitly to deliver. I have an amazing circle of friends, an amazing little boy, and by the time this book is published, I will have purchased my new townhome, will have a good job that pays for it all *and* is helping me clear some debt. I am a published author in an incredible series of books, including this one, and I am a contributor to a mama magazine. I will have left my nine-to-five job and will be running my coaching business full time, and if not, that's still okay. My time is coming for coaching full time, and I trust that with all my heart. It just means the time hasn't come yet for that venture to take off. But it will, and that's the best part. I know that I am the creator of my life and not a victim to my circumstances. Those circumstances have led me to this place. Life is pretty fucking good. The lemonade tastes delicious, finally. It is sometimes tart, but overall, it is refreshing and sweet. Much like the life and the blows we are dealt, it is up to us to make of it what we will.

A Dollop of Pleasure

The final lesson I have learned from my circumstances—the sugar in the lemonade to make it taste so sweet—is this: While I dislike my ex, I don't hate him anymore. For a long time I allowed the hate to take over me, and I couldn't see beyond all the bad things that he had put me through. Before I knew it, it permeated through every aspect of my life.

One of my favorite beliefs right now is that nothing happens *to* me, it happens *for* me. Without my ex, I wouldn't have my amazing little boy, and for that I am thankful and will forever be grateful to him. Without my ex, I wouldn't have found the world of life coaching. Without life coaching, I wouldn't have found my voice and love of writing. Without my ex, without that experience, I wouldn't have met some of the people I now call dear friends (even though we've never met . . . hello, online besties!). Without my ex, there would be no me.

I always used to be a-glass-half-full kinda gal. But lumps and bumps over the years beat that mindset out of me, and I was becoming more pessimistic and someone I didn't like at all. I can very happily say that my former self has returned, and she is happy with where life is taking her.

I have learned to care for myself, and more than just in providing for me and my son. I mean that I've learned that things like self-care aren't frivolous, fluffy things that are bantered about in the coaching industry. Self-care is something vital to my well-being. It is vital to our well-being. If we aren't filling ourselves daily with things that light us up, then we're doing ourselves a disservice. And not just ourselves, but our families and friends too. Self-care doesn't have to mean lofty things. It can be as simple as turning up the music and having a dance party in the living room, digging your toes in the sand, getting a pedicure, buying a little something for yourself, or whatever it is that makes you feel good.

Much like lemons and their tangy and tart yet sweet taste, life will have its fair share of bumps and bruises. Without them, we wouldn't be who we are, and we wouldn't be where we are. We need to still be able to see that glass as half full. We have to believe in ourselves enough to dig out of whatever rut we find ourselves in. We have to have the courage to choose better, do better, and be better for ourselves and those around us. We need to have faith in something much bigger than ourselves so we can stay open to possibilities and opportunities. They are all around us if we only allow ourselves to see them. Trust that the Universe will always support you, have your back, and lead you to where you are meant to be. Pause if you need to. Reassess and evaluate if you must but keep moving forward. Don't let the hard things beat down your spirit. And keep squeezing those lemons. You will eventually get some sweet AF lemonade. Just don't forget the sugar chaser.

chapter 6

WAKE UP TO THE REST OF YOUR LIFE

MICHELLE NICOLET

"But alas, the shovel of wonder, giving me the strength and courage of Thor, was still in my hand. My mouth continued to speak truth that had been suppressed for so long, and I just couldn't stop."

MICHELLE NICOLET

Michelle Nicolet wears many hats, including being a mom to four children. She is a medically released military veteran who climbed to Everest Base Camp and Island Peak, and she participated in the movie *March to the Top* as well as in Wounded Warrior fundraisers by cycling across Europe. Michelle is a recipient of the Queen's Diamond Jubilee Award, and she has served her country for the past thirty-one years in the military, public service, and most recently, with Veteran's Affairs as a Field Nursing Services Officer for Kingston, Ontario. During this time, Michelle suffered injuries from her service and second marriage. These challenges have served to strengthen and fortify her as well as to teach her to continually improve, learn, and evolve.

Michelle has a bachelor's degree in nursing from Ottawa University, a certificate in PeriAnesthesia nursing, and is currently working on her Real Estate license.

Michelle loves karate, and she took her youngest to train with her in Japan in 2017. Her kids are her heroes, and her dogs keep her company as she learns how to use her experience and knowledge to help others.

To my kids, Kane, Zara, Vanja, and Rhys. You keep the smile on my face, gave me strength when I didn't think I had any, and provided me with hope on days when I couldn't find any. Your smiles, your laughter, and your hearts walk with me every day, and I love who you are and who you are becoming. I love you for all the reasons, and I am so thankful for you each and every day. Continue to be you, trust yourself, and live on your terms. Love, Mom, Mum, Mummah, and Mother.

*"Forgive yourself for not knowing what you
didn't know before you learned it."*

~ Maya Angelou

wake-up call

/ˈwākəp ˌkôl/

noun

a person or thing that causes people to become fully alert to an
unsatisfactory situation and to take action to remedy it.[1]

By definition, wake-up calls aren't pleasurable, easy, or comfortable. I
mean, let's face it: Most people don't enjoy being woken by a blaring
alarm or being shaken awake from a deep slumber.

For a long time, I felt as though I were walking through my life asleep
but with my eyes wide open. It was as though I were living through a
horrible nightmare that I couldn't shake myself from, no matter how
hard I tried. The most difficult part about waking yourself up from a
never-ending nightmare? Facing the cold, often callous truth that has
now become your reality—the elephant in the room nobody wants to
talk about but that you know is there. Desmond Tutu said, "There is
only one way to eat an elephant: a bite at a time."[2] That is usually how

I eat my elephant—I select the hardest, toughest part and go to town.

So, there I was, standing outside on a freezing cold February night. My husband had just told me to make supper for him and the kids. He was sitting on the couch playing online poker.

Now, we had both had full workdays, but the underlying expectation was that when we got home, I was to continue working my butt off while he relaxed.

The truth is that for years, I have done just that. Tirelessly. However, this cold February night felt different. I don't know how, and I don't know why. You could say that this time the expectation was the proverbial straw that broke the camel's back.

Before I get into the details, let me rewind a bit. When my husband told me to make dinner, he also let me know that he would shovel some snow. I wasn't happy with the arbitrary way he decided which task each of us would do, how we would do it, and when it would get completed. To any outsider looking in and not knowing anything about my life or the dynamics within my relationship with my husband, this situation would have seemed like a simple method of dividing up the tasks, perhaps. At that moment, it could have been easy for me to think, *my cup has already overflowed, time and time again, so what difference does it make? Why take this moment to make a stand when it involves such a mundane task?* I have no idea why I didn't let it go. All I knew was that I was fed up with feeling like a second-rate human, like someone without a voice and not worthy of having their own opinion. I was tired of feeling less than, not good enough, and subpar.

So, I started shoveling snow, and surprisingly, I was happy. The air was fresh and crisp, I was moving, and nobody was relying on me or my ability to create a culinary masterpiece in thirty minutes or less with no preparation. I felt free, rebellious even, because I took control of how I spent my time and chose to do what gave me agency. Despite the anxiety that rolled through my belly, I still felt freedom, joy, and peace in my body as I continued to shovel away every bit of snow around me.

Pop! Like a daydream that had just burst, that peace lasted perhaps ten, maybe fifteen minutes. I could feel his presence as he came outside and stood directly in front of me. In my perspective, our dynamic was one where I was a subservient who was always told what to do and how to do it, which made me feel like this castle was my prison—I was never the queen of my castle, but always the cleaner, prepper, and fixer.

My husband said, "What are you doing?" *Strange,* I thought, *isn't it obvious?* However, my brain and mouth often do not coordinate their efforts for optimal outcomes. Instead, I said, "I'm sunbathing in the Dominican," with perhaps some humor in there and maybe a twinge of sarcasm. This evening, in my mind, felt so different than all the ones we ever had in our marriage. This evening, fear didn't circle the pit in my stomach. Perhaps anxiety had found a resting spot, but fear? No sign of it. My chest no longer had the dull ache of *what's next?* Nope, not tonight. Tonight, I had the shovel. My very own Thor hammer. What an odd amulet to hold, but it gave me the strength to say what I needed to say and stand up for myself for a change. I felt like for once, I was in control.

Or at least I felt in control for one wee second out of the thousands and thousands that had elapsed in my many years of marriage, leaving me feeling powerless more days than none. I was, as I knew I would be, the recipient of a tirade—one that I had experienced time and time again in the past—that I'm never good enough, no matter what I do. I knew this tirade as sure as the air I breathed. I also knew that me not making supper meant it would not get done, period. However, this time it was different. I knew it was coming, I was prepared for it, and somehow, I didn't allow it to stick to me and hurt me as I had done in times prior.

My children's ages at this time spanned a whole decade: ten, seventeen, nineteen, and twenty-two. They were perfectly grown, healthy, and capable of feeding themselves. However, years of conditioning returned that fear in my heart: *Oh, my God, maybe I am starving them? Maybe I should just go inside and make the damn supper?* But no, I had the shovel. Despite that, the words wouldn't flow the way I wanted them to. My brain and mouth were still incongruent. Instead, I said, "There is nothing wrong with you; you can make supper."

Had that been the only thing that I said that night, yes, that would have been sufficient. Had I stopped there, sure, our night would have been bumpy, but we would have weathered the storm. But alas, the shovel of wonder, giving me the strength and courage of Thor, was still in my hand. My mouth continued to speak truth that had been suppressed for so long, and I just couldn't stop. I was so happy to be expressing my truth for the first time in years. "And you know what? I'm done. I'm done with this marriage, I am done with you, and I'm out."

Yikes. I braced myself, thinking, *Holy f*%k, I'm in some deep shit now.* Still, instead of a sense of doom, for the first time in *years*, I felt a glimmer of light—let's call it hope. For the first time, I felt like I could live a better life, do better for myself, my kids, and our future. That I could leave. That I had a choice.

He had a strange expression in his eyes when he went back into the house. *Whew.* Well, no supper was made that night and when my ten-year-old asked about it, I took him and my seventeen-year-old out for pizza. It was just the three of us anyway, as my nineteen-year-old daughter was away at a friend's place for the night, and my son was away in the army serving his first mandatory three years of enlistment.

When we came back, the interrogation continued. This time it was because I hadn't told him I was going out for pizza. To my surprise and astonishment, shovel-less Michelle could also speak. *It must be the day; my moon must be on some planet whose aura is giving me more courage than I could ever muster alone!* I replied, very matter-of-factly, "Because you weren't invited," and I left it at that.

That night when he came to the bedroom, I asked him, "What are you doing?" He said that it was his bedroom, and he was going to sleep. I reminded him that I was serious about us being done and that he could sleep in the bedroom downstairs. And so, he went to the couch that night. Make no assumptions, though. A narcissist will not be defeated so easily. It's like playing a game of zombie apocalypse or something, forever ensuring you're armored up before the next zombie attack comes for you. In our case, it became a game of who-got-there-first. Whoever got to the bedroom first would end up sleeping there for the night. What a chore. What a pathetic joke. Tension filled our entire house, its thick discomfort permeating through every room so badly that you could choke on it or slice it with a knife. Personal strength and a constant awareness of having witnesses around were my saving graces through those months.

One morning I woke to screaming and spitting. Apparently, *I* hadn't done *his* laundry and he had to go to work. *Again, I don't know who this chick is, but she got some sass!* Thor-like Michelle told him, "Then do your own laundry. And for the record, make your own meals as well or move out." My then-husband's beliefs were rather antiquated in my opinion, and they didn't bode well for our marriage. I should state that I had still been making meals, doing the household laundry, and cleaning even after I told him our marriage was over. But now, those cleaning gloves were off, and they weren't going back on. Not for him. He lost his cool and therein began the typical tirade, once again. I knew this pattern and called the police. I met them a few streets away from the house and, upon talking to them, discovered that his screaming and ranting were irrelevant. They could only intervene if he hit me. For the record, he had hit me quite a few times before, but on this particular day, I was spared from his physical wrath. So, I could not do anything about it. I waited until I saw his truck leave for work and went back home. Life was so stressful during this time. We even had Children's Aid intervene and interview us and our youngest.

Have you ever been with a master manipulator? They put on a beautifully curated act for all the world to see. They are in performance mode—they do all the theatrics, perform displays of affection, and say all the right things. The same happened when the counselor came to our home. I felt like nobody would believe me. From what I could see at the time, it looked like the counselor was buying every word of his—how we were separating but living in the same home until it sold, how we care for our son, and though we may be going our separate ways, he totally respects me as his son's mom, etc. The lies continued to roll off his tongue. I was drowning with every word that came out of his mouth. I was being pushed deeper and deeper, and it felt so hard to breathe.

The next day, I got a call at work from the counselor who said it was obvious I wasn't safe in the home. I slumped at my desk, completely relaxed my once-rigid and guarded posture, and cried. I told her that I thought she believed all the words he had said, and she replied that her years of experience allowed her to see the truth. Oh, my God, the weight came off, and I could finally breathe. Oh, how glorious and yet painful that first big breath was. I felt like I had been holding so much in since her visit the previous day.

I was relieved, but it changed nothing. I still had the minefield to tiptoe through every day. I still had to be in the same house, for I had no place to go, and he refused to move out.

I still had to find a way to break free, from him and from the crippling debt and bills that continued to pile up. We had a home that was large and expensive. Guess what? Surprise! I found out that all the deeds to the house were solely in his name! I couldn't sell it or list it on the market without his signature.

He was asked to leave for the sake of peace. Meanwhile, for ten months, I was financially responsible to cover bills that were previously paid by two incomes. My lawyer couldn't do anything to speed up this process. At the time, given our financial woes, I also believed him when he said we could split amicably without lawyers. Fast-forward four and a half years, and we are still knee-deep in lawyers and court. But you know what? I am stronger. I lean into my belief that good things happen to good people, and I need to be strong and stay the course. And despite this turmoil, there are so many good things that have taken place in my life.

No matter the hardships, I trust myself to rebuild everything from the ground up. I know that to be true because there are accomplishments in my life that prove it. At the time, I had no idea that these accomplishments would be such a significant piece of my journey, but believe me, they are now. For instance, with ten injured soldiers in tow, I climbed Everest Base Camp and Island Peak in the Himalayas, which was a film documentary called *March to the Top*, supported by True Patriot Love. I spent twenty-two years in the military and served in Afghanistan. I have four children who are turning out to be fantastic humans. In 2019, I cycled with Wounded Warriors to Croatia, and to Juno Beach in France. I underwent two knee replacement surgeries, the latter to correct the first one that had been placed incorrectly. The grit, resilience, strength, and courage I gained through each of my past accomplishments are now the pillars that help hold me up. Every day, I remind myself that I am good enough. I am worthy of the love I give to others.

Though the journey has been physically, emotionally, and mentally exhausting, it is one that I have grown from and from which I have learned many valuable lessons along the way. I am no longer scared to admit that I'm afraid. I give myself grace to take a break, and when I feel down and out, I allow myself to reach out for support. Humility is grand and allows for so much.

The worst part of my past situation is how deeply it has affected my kids. Despite my best efforts to shield and protect them, I know they've felt the impact of living in a toxic household. I give myself grace and remind myself that none of us can be all and everything to them. They saw so much more than I ever thought, and as those emotions resurface for them, I do my best to hold space and be there for them. Our conversations are longer now and our understanding of and for each other continues to grow and expand.

My oldest, the guy who made me a mom, left the military after three years and only moved back home because I told him my ex had moved out. For eight years, my oldest felt the anger and hatred from my ex; nothing my son did was ever good enough. He is now relearning many aspects of our relationship. For a long time, he wanted me to end this relationship; however, from my perspective, it would mean a second divorce, a second failure, and a second stamp of disapproval from the world, and I couldn't do that. Until I could. We have come to accept each other's feelings and opinions and do what we can in this life, one year, one month, and one day at a time.

As you have read my story, perhaps you're wondering if I have managed to make a sweet drink of lemonade out of it. I'd like to say I have, and in many more ways than I imagined. Currently, I am in the midst of a messy divorce that is not of my choosing. There are days it feels incredibly scary to defend myself against the false allegations and navigate custody issues. But one thing is for certain: Nothing is scarier than the minefield I used to live in. Nothing is scarier than wondering when they are going to snap, when you are next going to face abuse, or not knowing when you are going to fully breathe again. Nothing is worse than losing my voice and expression.

Today, despite my ongoing challenges, I have freedom, and I have a life. Who would have thought that at the age of forty-nine, I would meet a very nice man and find love once again? A man who would know exactly what I meant when I spoke of walking on eggshells in a toxic relationship? Our relationship is so different from the minefield I escaped. We have real conversations, no matter the challenges we experience. It's so difficult to break patterns that have been ingrained from us at a young age through our childhood and prior relationships. I tend to freeze and shut down—my defense mechanisms. Meanwhile, he prefers to sit and talk it out. Well, I finally trusted someone enough to break the pattern. That's also my cup of lemonade. But I do have to say that I would not be with him if he were not so patient with me.

When I think of the old me, I laugh and cry so hard for all that she endured. At the same time, I rejoice for the woman I am becoming. I am proud of her and stoked for the next adventures. You see, I have shed more tears than I care to, but now, they are my choice to shed. Learning what is mine to own and what I cannot control have been some big lessons for me. I will never stop learning, laughing at my mistakes, and loving every minute of this crazy life. I am a daughter, sister, mother, and warrior, and I do make lemonade out of my lemons—you better believe it. I make my own choices, carve my own path, and set my own timing. Living life for me is glorious, freeing, and scary as hell. Don't let anyone ever take that away from you. Don't ever let anyone grind you down, for you are stronger than you think, bolder than you can imagine, and worthy of breathing and living your life as a sovereign, free being.

chapter 7

I MARCH TO MY HEARTBEAT, NO ONE ELSE'S

JENNIFER O'HARE

"Every woman deserves to feel empowered enough to change her mind, make her own mistakes, march to the beat of her own heart, and show up unapologetically in her full power."

IG: @JENNIFER01 | @LOVEMEFREEAMOVEMENT
FB: LOVEMEFREEBOX

JENNIFER O'HARE

Jennifer O'Hare is a multi-passionate individual. She is a loyal wife to her undeniably supportive soul mate, a mother to three small kiddos with larger-than-life personalities, an inspirational self-starter, an influential visionary, and a fun- and freedom-seeking enthusiast. Jennifer is a corporate retail merchant, a best-selling author, a columnist for *Mama Brain Magazine*, and a self-care accountability coach for women. In late 2020 she founded Love Me Free, the only subscription box for the "every" mom that inspires you to be your best self through premium products and a full-scope self-care experience.

To my sweet daughters and my lovable son for always bringing me back to zero. You ground me. My greatest accomplishment is and always will be raising all three of you.

"The greatest gift you can give yourself is letting go of other people's expectations for your life."
~ *Rachel Hollis*

From an early age, I craved massive amounts of freedom, independence, and connection. At the old age of four, I would sprint across the parking lot straight into my preschool classroom, only to announce to anyone who cared that I was there! At the age of six, I took it upon myself to get off the bus at my best friend's stop and invite myself over to her house as if I were old enough to make that decision on my own. Around ages seven and eight, my parents occasionally took my brother and me camping, and the first thing I always did was sniff out my new "friendships" before even unhitching the camper. In my double-digit ages, I often begged my parents to send me away to camp for the entire summer, only to be sent for two weeks. All this desire for freedom and independence paved the way for me to be a rebellious and somewhat naïve teenager who lived by her own rules, made her mistakes, and marched to her own drumbeat.

From the outside looking in, anyone would have thought, *wow, her parents must be super strict. That is why she wants to be out and about all the time or feels the need to break the rules.* Or perhaps they thought I was starved for attention, connection, and affection, which is why I relished in imaginary friends, frequent playdates, and experiences outside of my comfortable home. But that wasn't the truth at all. My upbringing was fairly traditional in the sense that my father worked long hours at a blue-collar job while my mother stayed home and raised her children, kept a modest but clean home, and made all the meals. My dad worked Monday to Friday (and occasionally Saturdays) and came home just in time for my mother's perfectly prepped meal, plated and set up just the way he liked it! Then, my family would play on the floor after dinner while my mother cleaned the kitchen. After the cleaning was done, it was time to bathe us kids. So, my mother would help us get clean and into our pajamas, then off to bed we went. Our weekends were always spent together as a family, and we would ride bikes, hike, or visit our lake house during the summer. My mother kept up her role of the primary caretaker even on the weekends while my dad did yard work or took a minute to sit down and catch his breath. We socialized with aunts, uncles, and cousins, and we often met up with my parents' friends and their children. Overall, my childhood was pretty ordinary and quite enjoyable.

From an early age, I was aware of the "roles" my parents played. My dad worked hard and tirelessly to provide financially for our family, and my mom worked hard and tirelessly to provide love and care. Both were undeniably committed on all fronts, but both also felt underappreciated and unfulfilled during various times. My mother took so much pride in all that she did for our family, but she often felt like her work was overlooked by everyone. She spent most of my elementary school years doing everything to make my childhood fun, exciting, and enriched, and she would often forget to do anything that made her feel the same way. My father worked so hard to build a business from the ground up and to invest in his passions like boating, summer houses, cars, and four-wheelers, only to never actively enjoy them! He spent most of my elementary and high school years telling me that owning your own business was mostly demanding and restricting versus freeing and empowering. Being a passive witness to these roles ultimately shaped my thoughts and views on how the world "must" operate: A mother and father must both work hard in their roles in order to empower and enrich their children's lives first. Then, when the children are older (and only then), they can begin to live their lives, dust off their passions, and create their own new identities.

Before all this conditioning was subconsciously ingrained in me, I was just a young girl full of life, personality, and charm, and being so genuinely curious and confident made me think that whatever happened in life and whatever mistakes were made meant the Universe was trying to tell me a bigger story. I understood the idea of "just being yourself." I honored individuality and creativity in others. I thrived in nonjudgmental friendships and in relationships with motivational teachers and coaches. I valued honesty, even if it meant voicing ideas or viewpoints that others considered weird or unconventional. My values were being created right before my eyes, and I was ready to come into the world with even more confidence as I entered my college years. I was ready to take on the responsibility of my own happiness and success and hopefully take away what I thought was a burden from my parents.

In college I participated in my fair share of parties, skipping classes, and thrill-seeking road trips, but I mostly felt aligned and clear. I knew who I was and how I wanted to show up in the world, and I did so unapologetically for four straight years. I felt alive and free and also fully in control. Upon graduation, I started doing some soul searching to discover what I wanted to do for a living. I knew I wanted a career so I could continue to support myself, and I didn't really want my education to go to waste. I knew I would eventually want a family, a house, and a white picket fence, and I trusted these would come when the Universe decided it was the right time. So, I dove into some "bridge" jobs until I landed the perfect career, and this career was designed just for me! It was everything I loved: fashion, travel, connection, creativity, variety, excitement, a fast pace, and just a pinch of structure to get me on my feet. I dove in, immersing myself in my role and career development. From the day I received that call about landing the job until the day I left for my first maternity leave, I felt more committed, passionate, and fulfilled than ever before. I met the man of my dreams, got married, bought a house, and had a couple of kids, all while working this incredible yet demanding career of mine. My support system was topnotch, and I was living my life according to my plan.

Like most people, my life changed drastically after having children. I finally understood how having kids can be your biggest accomplishment yet your biggest obstacle. I had an uphill battle with postpartum depression and postpartum anxiety during my first pregnancy, but I eventually learned to manage it by the time our second baby arrived. With the birth of each kid, the return to work from maternity leave felt incredibly hard. It was heartbreaking, but manageable. The drop-offs at daycare on a Friday after traveling all week would suck for a while and then the robotic voice in my head would repeat, "Jen, this is what every working mom goes through." Missing the preschool Mother's Day breakfast became "a thing," and I told myself that it would all be okay because "she won't even remember you weren't there, and you can just catch the next one." While I was acutely aware of the thoughts and emotions that circled my mind and soul with each of these missed experiences, I wasn't honoring them. Instead, I kept sweeping them under the rug and suppressing them so that they would magically go away. They just had to, right? After all, this is the life we all live, isn't it? The home, the cars, the two weeks' vacation, the marriage and kids, and the ongoing need to keep up with everyone else? But what about our own heart? Then, the Universe slapped me in the face and told me to start paying attention. When my second baby was around nine months old, I found out I was expecting another child. This wasn't in the plan! I immediately spiraled into perinatal depression and anxiety. Another baby? How was I supposed to live this life with another baby to take care of? So, once my second trimester hit, I convinced my husband (and myself) that we should put an addition on the house, fix up our basement for an au pair, and give this career-and-three-babies-juggling-act the old college try.

Well, hard and exhausting cannot even sum up what those weeks and months felt like. The job suddenly felt like a chore. The sixty-hour work weeks, the constant overnight travel away from my babies, the inflexible and forced work hours, the social pressure to climb the corporate ladder, and the lack of creative avenues one could take after having kids all caused some serious resentment on my behalf toward the job and everyone involved in it. I had stayed in my job throughout my first two pregnancies, but when I became pregnant with my third kiddo, I realized that my employment situation may not be serving me. To balance my lack of satisfaction with my career, I wholeheartedly threw myself into my role as a mother and a wife. I made perfect beds every morning and made perfect bottles and lunches. I wanted to be at every drop-off and pickup and at all the kids' social interactions (all despite having a live-in au pair). I worked out every day, I tirelessly tried to keep up a version of an intimate relationship with my husband,

and I tried my hardest not to disappoint friends, family members, and other close acquaintances when it came to outside obligations. And I did it all while traveling twenty-six out of the fifty-two weeks a year and having a husband who worked consistent nights. I quickly became a superhuman mom.

For a while, the accolades felt good. The applause felt good. Then one day, they no longer did. I could no longer keep up with the need to be perfect, to be superhuman, to be all things to all people. And just as quickly as I managed to climb high on the tower of perfection, I spiraled hard and fast into depression, burnout, and a full-blown identity crisis at thirty-five. I was losing weight by the minute, I couldn't stay asleep at night, and I was breaking out in mysterious skin rashes. And the worst part? I was constantly yelling at my kids and my husband over nothing. My body was clearly sending out SOS signals: *Jen, get a grip. Jen, slow down. Jen, come back to feeling free. Jen, enough. Stop trying to keep up with the façade. Jen, let go.* Still, despite those warning signs, I couldn't bring myself to stop. I was pouring myself into what I thought made me happy, but truly at the expense of my health. I went full throttle like I always did, then crashed and burned to the ground.

Once I hit my rock bottom, I knew something had to change. This was not me. I didn't recognize me. I didn't recognize the "victim" I was playing. The girl who once felt so confident, so strong-willed, and so fulfilled felt so insecure, so stuck, so depleted, and so lost. I had never been here before, and these feelings and emotions were new and confusing to me. I realized I had never really come across the right tools and resources or even the right mentors to help me walk through this hard time. I decided then that I would survey every mom I knew! I couldn't be the only one who felt this way; there had to be more. There had to be at least one person who felt how I did, right?

Most of the mothers I spoke to who were my age and in similar life situations identified with the emotions I was feeling. Many of them even went as far as agreeing with me by saying, "There must be more; there must be a way to be a successful working mother and still feel like you are 'there' for your kids while enjoying the amazing moments of motherhood." I spoke with my mother and many others who were from her generation. Most identified with the struggles and challenges working mothers face these days, and all of them admitted to going through some sort of identity crisis between the ages of thirty-five and forty-five. But the funny thing was that no matter what generation of mothers I spoke to, or even whether they were working or not, not one person had an answer. Not one person had the solution. In fact, they were either just as perplexed as I was as to how to "balance" the common struggles most mothers face after they are done having kids, or they threw their hands up and said, "It is what it is." This information was unsettling, and I have never been the type to accept something as status quo and shrug it off as if the problem doesn't exist. Thus, I was determined to reclaim my happiness, my fulfillment, and my joy and well-being.

I started pouring self-care into myself however I could. For the first time in a while, I created boundaries with everyone and stuck to them. I booked weekly therapy appointments and told my workplace I would be out of office during that hour. I said no to extensive travel and made sure to leave at five on the dot every day. At home, I released some control to others. I gave my au pair and my children more tasks. I blocked out times for my workouts instead of squeezing them in when it wasn't an inconvenience to anyone else. I started saying no when I truly didn't want to do something and yes to all the things I felt guilty about ever saying yes to before. I journaled and practiced mindfulness. I was invested in my mental, emotional, and physical health more than I had ever been in the last five years. And it felt so good. I felt like I could finally breathe without a weight on my chest. I felt free. I felt the fog clearing for the first time in many years. Slowly, I emerged from underneath the cloud of a hazy exhaustion and began to see things differently. I started feeling more inspired and bolder. I shifted the conversations with other moms from "Why does it have to be this way?" to "It doesn't have to be this way. There is more available to us, for us." I started to notice my worth—not just my self-worth but the value I bring to the table at my job. I showed up with more confidence, kindness, and grace at work and at home. I realized how much I have to offer the world and that making a personal impact was possible in so many ways.

With confidence came crystal-clear clarity. I knew I was meant to do something more. The little girl in me who grew up as a free spirit, adventure-lover, and social butterfly knew that I hadn't been standing in alignment. I had been conforming to society's ideals and modeling what I had witnessed as a child: *Work as hard as you can even if it's not fulfilling, and put your dreams and wants on hold until your children are older.* Nope, not anymore. I couldn't stand it and knew I needed to break free from these very ideals that confined my spirit. And contrary to my father's belief in owning your own business, I knew that the only way to do so was to pave my own way and create a transformation for others who needed what I needed all those years ago. I turned my very transformation into my dream business by blending my years of experience with my passion to make an impact in the life of every mother I possibly could. Every woman, every mother out there deserves to rediscover who she is and come home to her soul, again and again. Every woman deserves to feel safe and understood, to know that it's okay to let go of perfection, to not know all the answers, and to allow life and its serendipities amaze her every step of the way. Every woman deserves to do things that bring her joy, make her feel fulfilled, and give her both pleasure and purpose. And most of all, every woman deserves to feel empowered enough to change her mind, make her own mistakes, march to the beat of her own heart, and show up unapologetically. In her full power. And today, I created a business to bring back that freedom-seeking, adventure-loving, shamelessly confident and curious little girl—the one in all of us. To you, may you never stop seeking your joy, nurturing your curiosities, and tending to the very fires that burn bright within your heart. May you forever let who you are shine through and shine bright, even when it feels hard. Especially when it feels hard.

chapter 8

THE EARTHQUAKES THAT WAKE US

KIRSTI STUBBS COLEMAN

"Life is filled with seasons that must be honored—a season for unraveling, a season for cocooning, and a season of becoming."

KIRSTI STUBBS COLEMAN

Kirsti Stubbs Coleman is a mental health advocate, a personal brand coach, a coffee connoisseur, an intentional mama, and a woman on a mission. She is a corporate-ladder-climber-turned-entrepreneur who had that wake-the-fuck-up moment and never looked back. She embraces a simplified life and guides other ambitious, badass women in becoming intentional in their wellness, relationships, business, life, and parenting! A bold storyteller, Kirsti openly shares the juggle of motherhood, experiencing burnout, and how prioritizing real self-care allowed her to start playing bigger, better. Next stop in her journey to creating a more authentic and full life is beautiful Prince Edward County, Ontario, where she now lives with her two littles.

I dedicate this chapter to my kids, Stella and Mason. They are my reasons for living a more intentional life, and I am forever grateful for their nudges to slow down, to be present, and to play more. Never forget how badass you are! I also want to thank my mom and dad for their support and love. To Jeff: Let's never stop advocating for better resources and access to support for families living with mental illness—if we keep sharing our story, we will make an impact.

"You are here to decide if your life, relationships and world are true and beautiful enough for you. And if they are not, you must decide if you have the guts, the right—perhaps even the duty—to burn to the ground that which is not true and beautiful enough and get started building what is."

~ *Glennon Doyle*

I woke up four years ago, completely forgetting just how fucking badass I was. The truth is, I have done many bold things in my thirty-eight years here on earth. But life circumstances and adulting led me down "safer" paths, and after a few too many instances of doing what I thought I should do, I forgot just how brave I was. While in a meeting with my life coach, she suggested I write a list of my boldest moments to remind myself of my bravery. It was a simple activity that had massive ripples in my life. Highlights from that list include:

- holding a snake on my tenth birthday
- taking off solo to Australia at seventeen for a year-long exchange
- kayaking with killer whales
- moving across Canada "for a boy"

- asking for a promotion (more than once)
- speaking on big stages
- proposing marketing initiatives that cost tens of thousands of dollars
- cutting out toxic friendships
- having two babies under two
- saying YES to not one but two major HGTV home renovations
- leaving the corporate world to go all in on family and my own business

And those were just the big ones. In writing the list, I also realized that as a woman and mother there are often simpler, smaller moments throughout the day when we take bold action, yet somehow, they are rarely celebrated. Standing down a toddler who says none of their fourteen pairs of socks "fit right" comes to mind, or speaking up with a smart response to a clueless male leader at work who says something like "Well, if you are going to pay someone else to raise your kids all day, then you might as well work as hard as you can here, right?" Yes, that is from experience. WTF, right? I only realized in hindsight, long after the moment had already passed, how bold I was.

The best example I have of being brave, however, is the year I admitted burnout and subsequently took a medical leave from my corporate career. It was not in my plan. It was definitely not on my vision board or my carefully curated list of career goals. It wasn't something any of my friends had done or anything I had ever considered I would need to do. At the time, it didn't feel bold at all—it felt weak. We live in a society where the hustle is prized more than the authentic, natural flow of things. We are conditioned to think that asking for help is a sign of weakness or that we need to guilt ourselves into endless worry for taking time off to rest or slow down because our overall health and well-being is being affected by the nonstop race we run every day with no end in sight. And although every corporation has some form of "ask for help, don't be stressed, we care about your well-being," we keep going without fueling our tank, destined to crash and burn unless we make a bold move by taking a stand for ourselves. When my leave started, it felt scary, unknown, and uncomfortable. It also turns out stepping away from your job, which for me was my entire identity outside of being a mom, came with a heavy side of shame—the kind that needs therapy, Brené Brown books, and a few journals to navigate through.

From a young age, I learned that when you take bold action in your life, some people will get it while some won't. In the case of my leave, those closest to me were in disbelief and feared only for my career, financial losses, and reputation, thus making me feel unsupported and filled with shame. Once the shock wore off and I did the work to stop hiding my emotional, physical, and mental burnout, I let them in to see how I needed to rest. The moment I let them see my pain was the moment I remembered how brave and courageous I was to even prioritize rest and healing.

My burnout was a little over fifteen years in the making, so it goes without saying that healing would take far longer than the simple three-month leave of absence. This short-term leave cracked me open and allowed me to disconnect from people, technology, calendars, and professional responsibilities. I reached a level in my life I had never experienced before. My life until then was organized into a color-coded calendar. Disconnecting from it all was the scariest yet most life-changing decision I have ever made.

In these four years of healing, there have been lots of lows, small wins, huge surprises, and many bold "earthquake moments." You know, the ones that forever change you. They are the most chaotic and messy ones, the ones that shake you to your core and leave each moment forever etched in your memory. It's these "earthquake moments" I share with hope of bringing you light, laughter, authenticity, and inspiration for embracing the boldness we all hold inside us!

That time I lied to my naturopath . . .

I had been living in survival mode for a few years after having my kids when I finally decided to get serious about my health. At the time, I wasn't aspiring for whole health (shh, don't tell anyone I said that!). I simply wanted to be done with carrying the extra weight that sat on my frame and get rid of my excruciating back pain that continued to make its presence known (you'd think I'd had a third child right after my second). All I wanted was to feel good again in my body.

Back then, I thought I was nailing the idea of self-care. Sometimes, I would go for a walk, have a smoothie for lunch, and listen to a podcast on personal growth as I sucked back those expensive greens. On a good week, I'd even manage to have a bath on Sunday nights while I responded to customer emails. And, of course, I documented my bath and shared it with my online community to encourage their own self-care. I took vitamins when I remembered, I had pretty water bottles everywhere, and I even hired a personal trainer to work with me once a week between meetings. I had this art of self-care down to a science!

But it didn't matter what new self-care hack I added to my roster, it still felt like a heavy brick continued to press down on my chest. The weight of it kept closing in. The self-deprecation continued—for not drinking enough water, not responding to work emails quicker, not keeping the house clean enough, and so on. I felt like I wasn't enough as a wife, a mother, a friend, or an employee. I felt like I wasn't enough for myself.

Like so many moms, a large chunk of my days typically included most of the parenting and life stuff, plus more than eight hours a day of meetings for work and operating a small business online. Once, in a desperate employee assistance program call, a therapist had me look at time management and how I spent/allotted my time. Newsflash: I didn't need a forty-five-minute activity to tell me that I hadn't mastered time management. In this phase, my "not enough-ness" was pinned on my time management, and I was a resentful and angry version of myself that I didn't like. I remember when a well-intentioned colleague told me to look at a list of tasks I had made and then start crossing off those things that I could outsource or stop doing all together. I tried to, many times, and it ended with me in tears and not able to cross a damn thing off.

Deep within, I knew I wasn't well, and I hadn't been for a long time. Somehow, I thought my life was normal since every mom I met was just as tired, unhappy, frustrated, busy, and anxious as I was. At my lowest point, I hired help at home and had a significant amount of monthly therapy. It was becoming expensive to be mentally, emotionally, and physically exhausted.

Then I met Dr. Melanie. I had determined, after reading an article about the thyroid and stress, that meeting with a naturopathic doctor to do some further tests was a good idea. She was sweet and asked lots of questions. It felt a lot like therapy at first and nothing like a traditional doctor's appointment. After doing her initial assessment, she asked me how much sleep I had been getting. I laughed awkwardly and said something like "Well, if my three-year-old sleeps through the night, then about six or seven hours." She pointed her light into my eyes a second time, smiled, and said, "My guess is less than four hours, and I would also say it has been many months like this. Is that true?" Busted by a bright flashlight! How could she tell that by looking at my eyes?! I was eager for her to run some tests—no matter the costs—and then just tell me what to do based on those results. The quick fix. She had a different idea in mind—a slower and more gradual approach to health that met me where I was at the time.

For about eight months, she helped me understand the correlation between stress and my weight, sleep, self-care, and giving my body and mind what it truly needed. In that time, I went from coffee aficionado to once-a-day sipper, and I have maintained this new habit consistently over the years. I did acupuncture every few weeks and started to understand my disordered eating habits for the first time in my life. In many ways, I felt like a superhero as I made traction with my health, yet my personal life seemed to be hanging on by a thread.

That time I heard, "I'm fine. What's for dinner?"

It was a rainy June morning, and our tight little bungalow in the suburbs of Toronto was buzzing with the epic morning routine most parents can understand. It was barely 7:00 a.m., and I needed to get two small toddlers (ages four and two) fed, clothed, and out the door to Montessori with such fine execution that my husband wouldn't be late for the train downtown to his office, and I would miraculously arrive right back where I started—my home office—hair done, stylish outfit on, and creative juices flowing. Like some kind of mom-gician, I would be "ready" for an 8:30 a.m. call with a vice president who didn't understand why I wasn't able to meet in person, as I was "only 1.5 hours away from the office."

Today was a little different, though. Today, my husband would stop by the hospital for the results of his latest psychological assessment while en route to his office. He felt it was normal to carry on with his workday as usual, no matter the type of news he received. "It's not a big deal, Kirsti. They are going to tell me I am fine anyways and that you are making a big deal of nothing," he said, jeering at me with anger and snarkiness, taunting me with each word. Secretly (or not so secretly), my biggest fear was that doctors would find no issues whatsoever, and I'd be left without any answers for my husband's strange behavior. That I would have to live with continued uncertainty and emotional instability . . . with a critical man who was mean one day, emotionally distant the next, angry often for no apparent reason, and traveling for work anytime someone said go. I was often alone with the kids, multiple nights a week and one full week each month, all in the name of growing his career, while I carried the visible and invisible mother "load" day after day. Outside our home, I was the mom with a thriving career; I appeared to "have it all." But inside our home, it felt like a horrible time warp to 1955, minus the cute aprons and pastel-colored counters and wallpapered rooms.

That day, between my morning calls, I popped out to Starbucks for my usual "rough day" pick-me-up. With hot coffee in hand, I did what all happy, caffeinated moms do—I got back in my car, turned up the music, and sang loudly with the gusto of a woman free of children and worry! That is until I was interrupted by a phone call. It was my husband. I pulled over despite being a minute away from home. I will never forget how I felt, sitting stunned in my SUV with the rain pouring down, staring across the road at a beautiful Magnolia tree and listening intently through a broken connection and over the loud sounds of a streetcar on his end. He told me that he had received a new mental illness diagnosis. I asked him to come home, and he said, "No way! I am fine. What's for dinner?" Swooosh! Swept under the rug, just like that! It was his second serious mental health diagnosis since our daughter had been born four years prior, and this one came with new acronyms, things I had never heard of, and eighteen pages of notes that I would later digest every word of, wine in hand, once the kids were asleep. The answers I was seeking about his behavior should have been resolved, so why did I feel like I was cracking open Pandora's box? I was scared and felt so alone in processing everything. That day we received the diagnosis was absolutely an earthquake moment for me, but not for my husband. It would still be another year before he had his earthquake moment, which would include a full breakdown, shaking, and begging me to take him back home because he was afraid he would harm himself on his way to work.

That time it wasn't a business meeting . . .

The night I spent on the couch drinking wine and reading my husband's health assessment was the night when it felt like someone pulled one thread out of a tightly woven ball of yarn, and everything I held onto with a white-knuckle grasp started to unravel. Over the next two weeks that followed, I experienced my first panic attack while I waited outside at the Montessori pickup and my second moments after delivering an important presentation from my car so I could find peace during dinnertime.

My mentor and VP at the time reached out to book a coffee with me. It was just before the long weekend, and I was honored she was making the time to meet me. I remember thinking in advance about key projects I would share with her to give her a professional update.

I even tried to do my hair and choose a nice outfit. Perhaps she had a promotion or a new opportunity for me! I was excited. I was also very distracted, anxious, and in one of the worst seasons of my life, but I hadn't admitted any of that to myself yet. I had left the front door of our home wide open when I took the kids to school one day, and when I got home, nervously laughed it off. Mom brain, right?! So, that was where I was at.

In our "meeting," my VP shared how tired she felt between life, work, and kids, and the hectic pace she had to maintain. Immediately, I felt at ease. Then she looked at me and told me that we were not in a business meeting. She wanted to know what was going on with me. I gave the obligatory update on the kids and "life is busy with work" response. She didn't buy it. I uncomfortably added that things were difficult at home. I thought we would then switch topics, but she asked how the struggle was affecting me. No one had really asked me that before. I am still not sure why I did it, but I took a deep breath and proceeded to share how incredibly distracted and unwell I had become. It felt unprofessional to share this information with her, but I was so relieved to share it out loud. She cried with me. I remember trying to explain to her, through tears, that I felt like I was buckled into a train that was veering off its tracks so fast that there was no way to save myself and get out before it crashed. She reminded me that I am the only mom that my kids have, and therefore, I needed to "put my oxygen mask on first." It was powerful to feel seen and heard in my most vulnerable moments. She didn't let me leave the coffee shop without calling my family doctor, and she made me promise I would take some time away from work. I didn't even know that was a possibility for me. The relief that followed was a welcome release. What I didn't know then was just how much that conversation cracked me open. It was by far the scariest, boldest, and most life-changing moment of my life. For someone who had an hour-by-hour calendar from age seventeen to thirty-four, it was cathartic to disconnect from it all!

That time I heard, "Daddy has been sick a long time . . ."

There are no words to describe what it feels like when you hear those words from your kids. I was snuggled up close to my petite seven-year-old daughter in her equally petite bed. I reminded myself of the pep talk earlier—*Lean into the discomfort; all she needs you to do is hold space for her, Kirsti.* We then proceeded to write in her journal together, and I listened intently as she tried to make sense of her daddy's depression. I will never forget her looking up at me with her big brown eyes and telling me that she has known her daddy's been sick for a long time.

That day we had an overdue family discussion, in the simplest language we could find, about what depression is. We talked about how it is the kind of sick that is nothing like a virus. We talked about how it is an invisible disability and about how having a mental illness makes people feel and act. We even discussed the frustrating reality that nothing anyone else does or doesn't do can help someone with depression. I felt like we made our kids grow up beyond their years overnight; my heart ached for them. However, their father's mental illness and, most recently, intense depression, was affecting all family members—no matter their age or understanding.

That night in her journal, my darling empath daughter expressed sadness, anger, rage, confusion, and empathy. I have never been prouder of her in my life. We were both so present in the moment, and she was so raw. This experience of stepping out of my role as mother or friend and into the role of scribe while she passed through these emotions was so profound that night, that it changed me. It showed me that we can cultivate a deep understanding of the hardest moments and experiences as long as we lean into our heart and hold space for each other, or even ourselves.

It has been more than a year since we began doing this journaling exercise together—she speaks, and I write. As she talks about her fears, worries, hopes, and questions, I furiously write it all down for her. I am silent throughout, and no matter how hard it is for me, the only question I allow myself to ask is "How did that make you feel?" No matter what she feels or says, all I see is her bravery. I am forever in awe of the woman she is becoming.

That time I met my future self in a pair of red leather boots . . .

My eyes were closed tight. I could smell my hot coffee in the car console waiting patiently for me. My windows were rolled down, and I could feel the cool breeze off the lake and hear the waves and birds in the distance. A soothing meditation played through my earphones, but just like in the past four weeks, despite all my hopes for feeling present and calm, I couldn't get into it. I had been coming to this same spot by the lake every few mornings for weeks, and I naïvely thought it would be easy to teach myself visualization or meditation. I thought that by now I would have become a more Zen version of myself, but wow, was I ever wrong. It was not easy. The minute my eyes closed, my mind wandered to all the things. All the reasons I wasn't enough. All the daily details that gnawed at my mind. I couldn't stay in the moment, yet I was hooked on the peaceful ritual of coming to the lake. As if on autopilot, I found myself parked by the lake almost every day. Somedays, it brought me calm even if the mental chatter kept going.

And though I didn't feel very "Zen" through my numerous attempts at meditation, I kept trying, nevertheless. There had to be some truth to everyone who kept saying that meditation is a life-changing activity.

It wasn't until week nine that I experienced my first real, transformative visualization. After twenty-two intense minutes, I saw her: my future self, twenty-five years from now—where I lived, small details about what I wore, what my hair looked like, what my home smelled like, how I spoke, what I valued, and even what I served visitors. Most importantly, I had a clear vision of how I felt in my body and life. It was magical. And honestly, "future me" was SO BADASS that I didn't want to wrap up the visualization! Once I knew how to find her—this future self—I couldn't stop sinking into deep visualizations to connect with her.

The first time I let her truly guide me in making a decision in my present life was when I realized life could feel good, fun, and full of pleasure and desire. At the time, I thought it silly, but who knew a pair of red boots would be the accessory of choice that would forever change how I navigated all the ups and downs in life? I was at the mall late one night after the kids had gone to bed. I think I told my husband I needed to return something, but I went straight for the shoe store I hadn't visited in forever. I put on an expensive pair of beautiful red-wine-colored leather boots, and I was smitten. They looked amazing, and they felt so good! I had seen them a few times and had longed for and wanted them, but I'd never let myself try them on. After all, I had two kids in Montessori, car payments, a mortgage payment, renovation bills to pay off, vacations planned . . . *who was I to buy these boots?* They also looked nothing like the boots my friends wore—they were outside the standard mom uniform. My husband would likely call them "loud" but also love me for loving the loud boots. Beyond any of that, they felt so me. They gave me a certain confidence that was far more important than their cost or who else liked them. Then, I remembered a book I was learning from and the author, the amazing Tara Mohr, said to do small acts in the present that feel like something my future self would do.

So, there I was, in those boots, ten minutes before the mall would close, asking myself with my eyes shut, "What would she do?" The answer was loud and clear—*get the fucking boots, Kirsti!* I bought the boots that night. Then, I ran home and sold my kids old toys online to rid myself of guilt, and I never looked back. That rush I felt was not for spending a week's worth of groceries on shoes, it was from living my future self right here in the present. Me in the future was grounded, unique, bohemian, peaceful, calm, easygoing, and, most of all, fun! It felt so good to remind myself of my awesomeness every time I looked down at my bright, loud boots. Who would have ever thought that a pair of shoes could literally be the answer to it all? Right?! I stopped needing to ask for outside opinions as much—I felt confident I had the answers inside me. Life is funny, isn't it? These leather boots were what I dubbed "my work boots"—for doing messy work and building things—that helped me begin my process for burning down and then creating a new life that feels more beautiful, more simplified, and more ME.

But in all honesty, I realized in that moment that my future self was always available to me. I could always quiet myself down and choose to live from this space, make decisions from this space, and lead a life that felt as good on the inside as it looked on the outside.

There you have it. If these situations were ever measured on a Richter scale, I think there would be a tie. There have been moments that have felt like tremors leading up to these earthquake moments, and every single one of them was vital to my growth and healing. What I have learned during these years of waving the white flag on burnout is that self-love and self-care at its core is deep, messy work. Life is filled with seasons that must be honored—a season for unraveling, a season for cocooning, and a season of becoming. Much like earthquakes, each season will have its severity on the Richter scale. Some will leave you feeling gutted and devastated, while others will have you reeling, keeled over in every way, collapsing everything you knew to be true to the ground, leaving you no choice but to build yourself up the way you desire. And as you continue to pull yourself out of the wreckage and tend to the fractured parts of yourself, even the ones you never knew existed, you will see that deep within, you were whole all along. You needed to crack wide open, and even be broken over and over again, so you could build a stronger, gentler, and more resilient, aligned, and intuitive version of yourself.

chapter 9

HOW I STOPPED "OVERCOMING" AND LEARNED TO SIT WITH MY GRIEF INSTEAD

KAT INOKAI

"Loving my disabled body does not make me brave. But sitting with my grief? I'll take that one.
Yes. I think it's the bravest thing I've ever done."

IG: @BUMPANDHUSTLE
FB: KAT INOKAI, LIFE STORIES
WWW.KATINOKAI.COM

KAT INOKAI

Kat Inokai is a writer, content creator, advocate, and disabled mom of two who lives in Toronto along with her husband, Heath, and her dog, Rolo. She lives with multiple autoimmune diseases (Crohn's Disease, Hashimoto's Thyroiditis, Mixed Connective Tissue Disease, POTS—a form of Dysautonomia, Fibromyalgia, and spondylarthritis, among others), and she uses multiple mobility aids (cane, rollator, Alinker, wheelchair) to thrive. She is committed to dismantling ableism and gently educating those around her about identifying internalized ableism through sharing her own experiences in the digital space.

Since starting her first blog, *The Bump and Hustle*, in 2010, Kat has been a featured blogger for YMC and has had articles published in *Huffington Post* and *Metro News*, among others. She has also made appearances on radio and TV. She has written and spoken openly about miscarriage and grief, divorce and relationships, blended families, and chronic health and disability. She continues to chronicle her experiences on Instagram and at katinokai.com, and she explores many issues with guests on her podcast, *Let It Land*.

In 2018, Kat had a life-changing health experience that shifted her narrative forever and openly allowed her to identify as disabled. Since that time, she has immersed herself in the writing themes of healing, identity, accessibility, body image, and body acceptance, and has actively focused on creating content that openly explores self-worth and self-love through the lens of disability, while helping others to thrive and find joy along the way.

To my beautiful family who has given
me both roots and wings.

"It's no use going back to yesterday because I
was a different person then."
Lewis Carroll

Overcoming our challenges. That's the goal, isn't it? Learning resilience, adapting, and maybe even inspiring others in our wake? Breaking
through, getting over, pushing past, making something from nothing.
The triumph of the underdog. Pushing through every obstacle, crushing
it, landing on your feet no matter how hard the fall.

There is so much emphasis put on what lies beyond our recovery,
on what lies ahead of us, what happens *for* us, on seeking the silver
lining after something has caused us pain and hardship. If we could
just somehow transmute it, spin it into gold, and share the process of
how we did it, we would have reached "happiness."

We could be part of that inner sanctum who seem to have it all figured out. Heck. We could write that next best seller. We could be that
motivational speaker and "it"—that thing that happened to us—would
have all been for a reason, or better yet, that reason would now be in
service of helping others, would bring us success, and would somehow
now carry with it the balance of justification.

The way we make peace with our stories and the way we process them is vital to who we are. All the aforementioned is completely valid. I know there have been times when I've thought like that. However, one thing has started to become clear to me as well. The need and dependence that we feel to "overcome" is still symptomatic of our traumatized minds. It still shows the need for deep healing, for witnessing, and for community support. It still demonstrates the need for gentle compassion and tenderness as the need to achieve and "be" is dismantled and the walls come down. As we make space for our vulnerability, our grief, raw and unfettered, is finally allowed to pool before us.

As a disabled woman in this world, I know this truth deeply. I know that being present in each moment is a celebration. I know how hard it is to stay in the moment and make space for your feelings and healing when the pressure to "get over it" or "get better" or "keep going" or "push through" or "overcome" is inherent. The pressure to rebound in no time is breathtaking. It's exhausting. It's stifling. We punish our bodies for not being able to function "optimally," and we punish them to recover quickly. We moralize rest. We celebrate making ourselves sick with accomplishment. In fact, so much of what we know and root for in toxic achievement culture is steeped in extreme ableism, and that, in turn, is internalized so deeply by every one of us, able-bodied and disabled alike.

For years I added to my own internalized ableism. I fed it. I gave it one-liners in the morning such as "we all have the same twenty-four hours" when my body would spend ten of those wrestling with symptoms and chronic pain, four with doctors and medical administration, five with children, cooking, and cleaning, and the remainder playing catch-up with my career, all while plugging the holes in the dam with sleep because "I could sleep when I was dead." I was always in a race to achieve. I outsourced, but it just ballooned the scope of my projects. In my way I thought I could fast-track my business and make up for the time lost because of my multiple autoimmune diseases and complex health. Eventually, it all came crashing down.

It was a beautiful crisp March day, and we were all in the master bedroom, horsing around with the kids and their toy lightsabers. I wasn't exactly participating—more lying on my heating pad to soothe the joint pain that came with my Crohn's, mixed connective tissue disease, and spondylarthritis (I would be diagnosed with postural orthostatic tachycardia syndrome and several other conditions later)—but I loved seeing the gleeful battle.

Recently, I had some strange symptoms creep into the mix: numbness, burning, tingling, and extreme weakness in some of my extremities. I dismissed it as something mechanical, the result of nerves being pinched by one of my many bulging discs. It didn't seem too serious, but it had set a new tone to my discomfort.

After some exciting crashes and inadvertent rapped knuckles, yelps, and reprimands, the kids deserted my husband and me for their Lego. Heath looked at me, exhausted from his very invested refereeing, and I could feel his eyes linger on my face longer than usual.

"Honey? Did you get hit with a lightsaber when I wasn't looking?" he asked.

I went to say no, but my tongue felt thick and strange in my mouth, my lips like rubber. I slurred as I started to speak, so I closed my mouth, hoping to regroup and try again. I couldn't speak. I looked at him, perplexed. Heath grabbed a small decorative mirror I kept on my dresser and brought it over to me.

The right side of my face was drooping severely.

"Can you lift your arm?" he asked.

I could feel my thoughts transmitting the signal; I could feel gravity jamming it hard.

I couldn't move.

Oh, shit. Was I having a stroke?

The weirdest thing about emergencies is that we try and plan for them. They are by very definition situations that simply emerge with great urgency. There's an element of unpredictability that sticks to the word. So, why do we as humans—and I'll zero in a little more and say, why do we as women, caregivers, and mothers—try and prepare for them relentlessly? Why do we constantly seem to be in a state of anticipation?

No amount of my worrying and ardent contingency planning could have prepared me for what happened over the next hours and days. I certainly did not know that when my kids hugged me good-bye, terrified that "something was wrong with Mom," that I wouldn't see them for almost thirty days, and that when I did, the only life-or-death drama they'd be concerned with would be who got more of the grape Jell-O on my dinner tray at the stroke/neuro rehab facility where I was living.

Life in its impassioned ups and downs is extremely odd.

It turns out I did not have a stroke.

I did, however, have an atypical, stroke-like neurological reaction to one of the medications I was taking—an injectable biologic helping treat my Crohn's and sacroiliitis. For many days I couldn't lift my right arm. I couldn't sit up. I couldn't walk. I had extreme weakness in my legs, along with paresthesia. I had to learn to walk again, moving from wheelchair to walker, to rollator, to cane. I had extreme difficulty swallowing and choked and aspirated everything. I was put on a dysphagia diet. I worked with a speech therapist. I couldn't see properly. My brain felt overwhelmed by processing too much stimulus at once.

I couldn't remember the next steps in simple tasks. I worked day and night with doctors, physical therapists, and occupational therapists to gain back my strength and to develop strategies for the cognitive and dysautonomic effects this episode had left me with.

And my motivation? I was going to go home and ***get back to my life.***

I was going to be the best version of me yet.

In spite of it all, I was going to heal. No one would ever see what I had been through.

The day I left, the nurses on my floor cried. Now, I can't help but remember this time through the lens of their experience. I know now that in part they were crying because they knew what was yet to come. I hugged them tight. I bought them coffee and their favorite donuts, and they each squeezed my hand through the window of the car before I left. I felt like I had graduated summa cum laude. I had learned so much about myself. About resilience. About listening to my body.

I had learned about how adaptive our minds and bodies can be, and I was so proud to have learned to use the mobility aids that would let me thrive. I was proud that I had adaptive strategies for cooking, for cleaning, for avoiding falls. But as we pulled away, I felt ice-cold panic. There were no strategies to reintroduce myself to my kids and family or to my world. There was no way for me to say, "Hi, I'm still me, only I'm completely different now." There was no pep talk or session to talk about the surprising wave of grief that would follow me from this nurturing place of care to the place where I was the caregiver.

Home.

I remember feeling like a ghost of myself when I finally walked through my front door. I knew that my husband and in-laws had cleaned and tidied since I had left, yet somehow, all my things seemed like artifacts, their contexts long gone. Nothing was mine, it was all hers. They belonged to the Kat of last month. The one who juggled chronic illness, and kids, and work, and relationships, and managed to keep the fine veneer of presentation intact no matter how much she was falling apart.

That Kat could whip up strategies for clients in her sleep. Complete production and financing rollouts would come to her overnight. No really, she'd keep paper and a pen by her bed at all times. And aside from work, that Kat never forgot to sign forms for field trips, or pack lunches, or make dinner. She even had spare birthday cards squared away "just in case." She had entire drawers of "just in case." And I had no idea how to relate to her anymore.

When I was alone, the unrelenting questions of my mind became louder and louder, and in response, they found the equally deafening silence of not knowing. I had lost myself. When I was with my kids and my husband, I was perpetually trying to show them that I was okay, to offer them the reassurance that I wasn't going anywhere, and to be a model of motherhood and safety. When I saw family and friends, I felt trapped between the role of a hero and anecdotal victimhood.

I was exhausted.

I knew I needed acceptance and normalcy again, but I also knew that I could only create that by moving forward and embracing even more discomfort and growth, and I wasn't ready to stop being everything that I had curated my identity to be.

I couldn't gently dowse the new path ahead without letting go.

I told myself I didn't have the energy, but the truth was that I wasn't ready to grieve.

"You're so strong."

"You're so resilient."

"You're such an inspiration."

Inertia can be seductive.

I didn't want to move ahead, and I didn't want to be stuck in the past, and the stillness of nondecision was comforting.

"You're so inspirational."

I clung to those words. I needed them. I grew dependent on them. I soaked them up like honey.

Months passed and I moved further from this trauma experience that anchored my new identity as "She Who Overcame," but I felt the effects of its withdrawal sharply. I kept looking to reconnect with the pain that I experienced, so I could overcome it again. I tried to find opportunities to stay relevant in this new world, to speak about what had happened, to establish that I had, in fact, made progress, and to state that I was proud of myself and the many things I had accomplished since my time in the stroke/neuro ward.

My identity felt blurred. Distorted. I craved definition through what I could achieve now with my disabilities, but the only yardstick I had for measurement was that one month of my life that I spent in the hospital learning how to walk again. Slowly, the timeline of my life seemed to disappear, all except for my heroic story. It's like the person I was before this experience was irrelevant. I never talked about my love for producing and filmmaking anymore. I didn't talk about blogging or acting, or writing, or music, or the years of business and design consulting I had enjoyed. I didn't stop to reminisce about my favorite memories as a child, or as a mother. I didn't even stop to process that this one experience was, in fact, part of an infinitely larger picture of my individual biology, of my health, of chronic illness, of my environment.

I need to clarify here, and I alluded to it earlier, that I think it's natural to let certain defining moments shape your life, and this one certainly shaped mine. I also think it's important and powerful to share those stories. They can help people so much. Stories can connect communities, provide support, and give hope. I know that my story resonated deeply with others every time I told it, but the way I was telling it kept building me back up simply to break me again. It engulfed me more deeply each time I shared it.

My anxiety—that had been manageable for so long—started to resurface. How could I shrink down and be that one story again and again?

My anxiety was also quick to point out the benefits: It was so clean and simple. All I had to do was polish that one dimension over and over again, and I would feel safe and comfortable forever.

And when I told the story like a story, complete with the "Once Upon a Time," and the perilous danger, and the ending where love and resilience conquer all, my family felt safe too. It was almost as though if I kept repeating this story over and over again, it would metaphorically turn back time and perhaps preserve the version of me that no longer existed so that everyone around me could feel safe, supported, and stable, and as if nothing had changed. Yet everything had changed. I was the brave protagonist, and it was a finite adventure—something absolutely wild that happened once and could be filed away with equally wild memories, like the time they thought they saw a UFO, or the time that my husband made us all inadvertently cut through a Floridian park populated with snakes and alligators.

They didn't have to see it as something that could happen ever again. Mom was safe. If my story was wrapped up as a fairy tale, they didn't have to process the fact that my health was becoming progressively more complicated or be reminded that my being in the hospital was something that occurred far more often than wrong turns during an evening walk in Orlando.

I was feeling this big, juicy, fear-driven existential crisis because between those parentheses, life felt so safe and comfortable. I was terrified to evolve beyond my phoenix-rising-from-the-flame story because, after all, wasn't being that person the goal? If I evolved beyond it, who would I become? What other life experiences would I have to go through to keep the love of those around me?

That frozen feeling went on for months—through countless social media posts about mindfulness and parenting, and how I was managing to get through it all; through more accolades that now felt empty and cold in my gut.

I remember turning to my husband after the kids were asleep one night, quaking hard, telling him that I had lied about everything for what felt like forever, that I had done everything imaginable to distract me from myself and to avoid this moment of just sitting and feeling. I let the raw, uncultivated, unedited story flow from my heart. It was the moment of sharing my "shaken to the ground" truth.

That admission set things in motion, but the processing is still underway. Even as the words you are reading first came to me, I was trying to control and curate my life. I wanted to see a highlight reel in print, to put parentheses around one of my worst experiences and one of my most dramatic recoveries, then feel the praise of "overcoming."

I thought I had found a way to tell the world that I was disabled, but I was strong.

That I could be inspirational.

That my potential wasn't limited, even if my body was.

I wanted to write and be published so that my family could see that I was truly worthy. I wanted them to see that I had achieved something, even though I was navigating through chronic illness symptoms and disability.

What I know now is that this was my way of wanting to be accepted; that the very motivation I had tapped into, with its charismatic momentum, was part of my own internalized ableism, and that the real story I had to share was not how I learned to walk again after leaving the stroke-neuro ward. It was not about reconnecting with my family through my recovery.

It was exactly this story—not of overcoming, but of dismantling.

How I started loving and accepting myself enough to realize that my hero narrative was utter bullshit.

How I realized that being in my body does not make me a hero.

That allowing myself the time and space to rest and heal does not make me a hero.

That using mobility aids does not make me resilient.

That doing everyday tasks with my family in my disabled body does not make me inspiring.

That loving my disabled body does not make me brave.

But sitting with my grief?

I'll take that one.

Yes.

I think it's the bravest thing I've ever done.

Once upon a time there was this amazing disabled woman who allowed herself to unsubscribe from achievement culture. She didn't make lemonade when life gave her lemons because she didn't feel the need to make anything at all. In fact, she ordered in instead. But she did make space for her grief, check in with her traumas, and dismantle her internalized ableism one breath at a time, all with her family at her side. She didn't overcome anything. But she did keep moving through whatever life brought her, over and over again. And that seemed just as good.

chapter 10

THE BUCK STOPS HERE

TONI RONAYNE

"Motherhood is an oxymoron. It's a blessing and a sacrifice."

IG: @THEDOLLHOUSERENO
FB: TONI.RONAYNE
WWW.TONIRONAYNE.COM

TONI RONAYNE (SHE/HER)

Toni Ronayne is a visionary leader, culture champion, mother, and advocate. She believes in the power of connection through authenticity and challenges cultural norms about how female leaders need to "show up" in the corporate world, and she champions that vulnerability is a strength to be shared. Toni is the co-founder of H20 Canada, a charitable initiative that provides clean water and sanitation education to villages and communities in Eastern Africa, and she uses her privilege in the mentorship of others. As a global executive, she has traveled to the far corners of the earth to grow talent and industry across five continents.

Toni has committed herself to living a life of "yes," which has opened a multitude of experiences. In this vein, she took on her greatest growth experience in her new role as a mother when she and her husband adopted their three daughters. She now devotes her life to loving and supporting her strong and beautiful children as they bloom and grow. Toni is passionate about advocating for families to overcome the archaic methods that exist within the system, to reduce the layers of trauma that adoptees experience in their lives, and to challenge the systemic beliefs that "adoption is a fairy tale." Toni's new personal ambitions now involve becoming an author, moving to the countryside, and restoring the 1800's Victorian farmhouse of her dreams.

To our strong, beautiful daughters who light up our lives and teach us something every day. You have given us such purpose. To Owen, my husband and best friend, thank you for holding my hand every step of the way. To my mom and dad, thank you for your support, your sacrifices, and for always showing up with unconditional love. And to the incredibly powerful community of women in my life, I see you, I love you, I applaud you, and I appreciate you!

"Love is the strongest force the world possesses
and yet it is the humblest imaginable."
~ *Mahatma Gandhi*

A love letter to YOU, who was, is, and always will be mine:

You were born to me. You were meant for me.

You have been with me every day, every hour. I have forced you beneath the surface to be tended to only when I have a tender heart. You chose me. You chose me to have the gift of your life, your end . . .

I have grieved, on most days alone and in solitude. You were my baby.

You were the little girl with curly ringlets and a generous smile. You were the one who would defy the odds set against you. You were the one who would set my life on a different path. You were my baby. You are my baby. You always will be.

I felt your presence in my body and in my soul in the earliest moments of your life. You were the sweetest, kindest, warmest soul. It was easy to give up everything for you because you were meant to be mine. To say that I could recognize your gifts at the time is a lie. In the literal sense, I believed you were a gift from God for me—despite those closest to me who deemed you nothing more than a disruptor—a problem, a barrier to my life, a mark on my pureness . . . a distraction from the ideals of what my life was meant to be. I accepted you and all the consequences that would come to be. I was prepared to weather this storm with you, with us, together. We were a team.

Born of sin, a derailer to our lives, and a distraction from our future—you were easy to forget for the people who claimed these things. And for those I would encounter over the years, you were nonexistent.

Your death caused great mourning and extreme pain. The loss of you was physical, graphic, and traumatic. I will never be able to unsee the events, nor will I be able to wipe away the sordid, raw, and painful memory of that night. What a swift and undignified end to your precious life.

Thank God I had courageous parents who mustered the strength to give us the simplistic gift of dignity in those moments, and who were capable of loving both you and me. Those minutes felt like hours, and the hours felt like days. You were gone, and there was nothing I could do to change it. None of my efforts, beliefs, or strength could bring you back. You were to be my legacy, and you were gone forever—your absence haunting me and gnawing at my soul, every fiber within my body feeling empty and alone again.

I have never received more love from my family than I did in the moments of your death. While it "was the right thing to do," they showed me their ever-present courage and resilience. They comforted me and slowly helped pick up the pieces of a very shattered me.

We buried you that night. Every time I drive home, you are there. I know that you are buried in that little box underneath the tree. Every winter you are covered with snow, and as the snow melts, you bless us with flowers and the beauty that is to be enjoyed in the coming months. Your presence is special. It always has been. You are there for all of us to enjoy in the physical sense, but your connection is so much more meaningful for those of us who know your story. In the spring you shine your beauty for the neighbors. The magnolia flowers bloom for everyone to admire. For us, though, we remember you, we reminisce about what came to be and what we lost. The simplicity of our lives was abandoned, and yet we are still greeted by a comforting reminder of you every spring, in your glory. We are grateful for that.

I lost you on the fourth of September. No doubt by the sixth of September, I was back at work. Luckily, people were kind and likely spread the word not to ask me about you so life could go on. It was incredibly difficult to exist in a world of fake interactions and pleasantries, but deep down, I knew that it was the kindest thing for those around us to do.

You have not been defined by your death. In fact, you have always been with me—ever-present and always guiding and loving me from the other side. You have given me the strength to face what's to come and have comforted me in my times of need. You have taught me how to be kind, to empathize, and to love. You have allowed me to see that strength, love, and patience can be born from vulnerability. You have prepared me to be a better mom than I ever could have been to you.

It's taken me seventeen years to talk about this tragedy, and I know why. It's guilt—guilt that has been ingrained in our bones, our spiritual bodies, and in our psyche. Guilt that has been projected onto us by the chains that bind us together. It's the confines of society and its unnerving, hypocritical, patriarchal standards.

It's about the "value of the loss." Whose loss is greater? *Hers or mine?* By societal standards, we have been ingrained to only value what is tangible and seen versus what is known and unseen but felt immensely in our hearts and souls about the value of life. To meet a woman who has lost a child (regardless of the circumstances) is to meet a woman who has grieved that child and feels responsible for the loss.

No doubt this truth is difficult to realize. That's the beauty of ongoing societal and marital pressure—the never-ending expectation for *me* to "be happy" because *time has passed, it's been so long,* and *it's up to the woman to nurture her home both emotionally and mentally.* And here's the kicker: I wore that expectation very well. I dressed to the nines, no matter where I went or who I interacted with—friends, family, colleagues, even a stranger in the grocery aisle. I was the perfect convincer, to myself and others, that this loss was "meant to be" and my life would be better for it. It was easy to persuade myself that I was too young, too naïve, too "everything." In some ways these statements were true, so it made it easier for people to move on and pretend like this loss never happened. Everyone around me (with the exception of my own mother) was ready to forget. But for the last seventeen years, I have sat alone on September 4, memorializing this ideal child—connecting with her, grieving her loss, and apologizing that I was not "woman enough" to carry her to full term.

That's the thing with grief and loss: It just is. Life doesn't slow down, nor should you want it to. So, I continued to honor your memory in my heart and soul every single moment, and I also traveled the world, invested in my career, lived between two countries, and fell in love with the love of my life. Together we found great joy in the success of our careers, bridging our families, making memories, and sharing laughter in a house that we would eventually "grow into." We became a unit—totally unstoppable, the #dreamteam, #couplegoals—the type of couple that people idealized. We were full of charm, charisma, and success. I threw myself into work and sought out any opportunity to get involved in making a difference for others, be it charitable work, personal mentorship, or the need to be in the driver's seat of a business. In many ways I soon became an inauthentic version of myself. I was a master at helping others realize their dreams while shelving my own dreams and needs away. I thrived on being the "fixer"—I was addicted to fixing everyone's problems but my own.

On the outside, I had it all. On the inside, I was burnt out and neglecting my inner voice and the voices of those around me who told me to "slow down" or "put myself first." And I am confident that it was my insatiable desire for control that prevented me from being vulnerable and open-hearted, especially when my husband wanted to start a family.

Over the years we discussed our desire to become parents, and for a while, I threw myself into trying. I approached it as if I were running a business. I developed the "business plan" to set up time for intimacy and to track my ovulation. I silently bought pregnancy tests at the first hint that my period may be late. As always, the results were negative, and slowly but surely, my heart hardened. I struggled with feelings of inadequacy. *I couldn't give a grandchild to our parents because I was physically broken. I was not "good enough" to be chosen as a mother. I was being punished for something that was outside of my control.* The stories I spun would be the demise of me. Surely, I was to blame for all of it.

When the questions died down, it felt easier to let go of the desire to have a baby. I began making excuses for us. My husband didn't want to try, and I didn't want to subject myself to fertility treatments. If God didn't intend for us to become parents, then we should just be grateful for the life that we had. We had everything going for us except *that*, so shouldn't we be satisfied? Certainly, becoming parents was not the holy grail of our life's purpose! I began convincing myself that we would be happy without children—some things are not meant to be, after all. And ironically enough, the Universe was lining everything up for us to start the next phase of our lives.

We had been considering moving overseas to live with my husband's mom for quite some time and doing so felt like the next best step in our life plan. I was achieving success in my career and was fulfilled. I was traveling the world, taking quick trips to Europe and longer trips to South America and Australia. I was shattering the glass ceiling as a female executive in a room full of men, providing business advice that created a profound impact. My husband and I had an incredible amount of freedom, and we enjoyed the fruits of our labor.

This was our life, and we had gotten used to it. Then, we started to plan the next phase and began the process of throwing ourselves into the details—evaluating the house, speaking with realtors, fantasizing about our new life, telling our friends and family about the move, and seeking the support of our employers. Without abandon, we mapped out our plans for the next ten years and started idealizing our future. We finally "had it all," or so we thought at the time.

In the blink of an eye, everything changed. Right before I was set to depart for another business trip, my husband received a call that would change our life trajectory. He was contacted by one of his long-term colleagues, inquiring whether we would be open to adopting three of his granddaughters. While we had loosely talked about adoption, we had not taken the natural steps to understanding what it would entail. We also had little information about the girls aside from the knowledge that they were under the care of people from outside the biological family.

My brain immediately swelled with curiosity and questions while I grasped for control and knowledge—I wanted to understand anything and everything about these children. *Were the girls healthy? How old were they? What trauma had they faced? Three girls? What are their names? Were we even capable of being parents? Would we be accepted? Were we worthy?*

Naturally, my response was something to the effect of "shock and awe." My husband did not require any of these answers, however. He was already convinced that this possibility was something we needed to take seriously—this was our time—our opportunity to finally "become parents." We were being given this chance, and it was up to us to choose to take it and make the most of it. Historically, I have been the "spiritual" one in our relationship, believing that all things are intended and being quite open to walk through a door because it "feels right." My husband, on the other hand, has always been steady and more strategic about balancing emotional decisions with logic. Not this time, though. This time, with the openness of his heart, he was "all in." He was rewriting our future after one phone call and expected me to echo the same enthusiasm. I wanted that too but was paralyzed by my own fear. Could this really happen? Was I going to take a chance and then suffer another loss?

No longer was I an open-hearted, idealistic woman. Instead, time and experience had hardened me, making me cautious and pragmatic. I continuously sought to keep myself safe from the threats. Yet in a matter of days, we decided to adopt our girls. When we met them, it only took moments to fall in love and know that we would give up everything for them.

The coming days and months would prove to be arduous as we navigated the process, bonded as a family, and shed the identities of our former selves. There is no book or seminar that can prepare you for the challenges that you will face as an adoptive parent or the trauma that your children will face having to be "placed again" in a new home. Adoption is not a fairy tale, and contrary to what the society believes, we did not "save our children." We have consciously chosen to love one another through some of the most transformative and challenging days in our lives. In our family we are all equal and supportive of one another on our spiritual journey in this life.

As parents, we have decided that as we go through this life together, we keep no secrets. Honesty and transparency are critical to ensuring our girls have the clarity of their identity and the safety to explore their biological history before my husband and I became their parents.

The fabric of our family is rooted in honesty and raw and real vulnerability as the girls become more actively interested in learning about our lives. While we spend most of our time focused on supporting them through their needs, our girls often ask us about our lives before they were ours. They ask lots of questions about the memories that they were not able to share together with us.

"Tell us about your wedding."

"When did you and Dad meet?"

"Who gave me my name?"

"Tell us about when you were kids."

One night the girls asked me, "Mom, did you have any kids before us?" I shared the story of the little girl in my tummy who now resides in heaven. Naturally, I gave them a brief story to satisfy their curiosity, but I kept it honest. I also let them know that sometimes God decides when people are meant to be parents, and that we were given the gift of being their mom and dad—we were chosen to be together in this life. We transitioned into a discussion about how we came to be a family and the struggles that we all faced before our time together, and we finished the night with some teeth-brushing, laughs, and bedtime stories.

I truly believe that this life was all part of my intended path. While I couldn't see it back then, the timing was right. We required the time and the experiences that we were given so we could be prepared for the beautiful opportunity that awaited us when we received that phone call. While we would have loved to have been younger when we became parents, our experiences have led us to overcome the challenges that many adoptive families face and enabled us to provide a home where our girls can thrive.

I am grateful for the tall order that we have ahead of us, and for my angel who guides us on the other side. It took me seventeen years to finally grieve my loss, to give myself the grace to acknowledge that my motherhood journey began all those years ago, and to recognize that though my little girl may not be with us physically, she has been with me the entire time—guiding, guarding, holding, weathering all the storms, and celebrating every success. All the grief, work, and love guided us to this moment: We were meant to continue this journey as parents to our three little girls.

After losing a child, a woman is full of pain and loss. Yet this pain and loss is borne alone, deep within herself. She works hard to forgive herself for her feelings while endlessly picking up the pieces of a family unit that is now fractured. Sure, the fracture will heal over time, but the dull ache will still be there, echoing its pain on significant days, memorable occasions, and sometimes, in the simplest of moments. Thanks to years of societal conditioning, the natural thing for her to do is to retreat, move on, and continue with what was "normal" before this significant life event. As women, we are often fighting to prove our strength; we are always living to prove and convince ourselves and others that everything is perfectly peachy in our worlds. Often, this fight means hiding our personal burdens and being a source of strength to serve those around us. We set unrealistic expectations for ourselves, which results in an unnatural balance when the chips are down. When a woman suffers a miscarriage, there is an expectation to move forward, move on, and survive as soon as the child dies. This expectation is how stigma is born. This stigma is generational, and as a mother of three girls, the buck stops here. Loss is loss, and every person has the right to be vulnerable and grieve without judgment.

Motherhood is an oxymoron. It's a blessing and a sacrifice. We are the "providers of life" for our children, but we can often neglect ourselves along the way. With the way of the world, we are mothers, teachers, executives, entrepreneurs, and "the safety police," kissing boo-boos and trying to create a sense of normalcy in what is an unnatural world. We all have unrealistic expectations of ourselves, and we need to teach our children that "doing our best" is good enough. Let's give ourselves the time, space, and grace to breathe, make mistakes, and shed our own ideals about how a "good mother" shows up. Let's take the time to find the joy in the mundane and love without abandon. Let's allow ourselves to openly feel our sorrows and unapologetically feel our way through life. Share your vulnerability and create a space of love that is without fear or retribution. Take the time to heal, with no judgment of your process, and share the story with your children. What you will find is that they will love you beyond the bounds of your own heart and will teach you a thing or two.

chapter 11

NAVIGATING GRACE WITHIN LOSS

MICHELLE TONN

"You get to choose what heals you. Hold onto whatever makes you feel alive. Hold onto what brings you hope. I do. Because I'm learning to love myself, while finding myself at the same time."

IG: @EMERGENCELIVING | @THEEMERGENCECOACH
WWW.EMERGENCELIVING.COM

MICHELLE TONN

Michelle Tonn is an educator, creativepreneur, and two-time best-selling author who is embracing the beautiful art of story-telling. In late 2017, she made a heart-centered leap to launch her own copywriting business, Emergence Creative, and foray into the depths of writing in which she shares her struggles and triumphs. Utilizing her background in business management, part-nership development, and education, she has grown Emergence Creative into the lifestyle brand, Emergence Living. She provides mindset coaching and empowerment to women who want to embrace their heart's desires, shift dialogues, and love themselves. Join Michelle on her journey as she infuses thoughtful intentions into future collaborations in hopes of igniting a spark within you to create a sense of belonging and serving with purpose and authenticity.

To the one who inspired it but will not read it. You are a beacon of light in my pursuance of light and grace.

Grief can be the garden of compassion. If you keep your heart open through everything, your pain can become your greatest ally in your life's search for love and wisdom.

~ Rumi

We walk along the wild west coast with the waves of the Pacific Ocean lapping at the shore. Your long red hair is pulled high on top your head and whips back and forth with the wind. My feet sink into the sand as I listen to your laughter and sarcastic retort to something I said that was uncharacteristically cool. Lifting my face to the sun, I close my eyes and inhale the salty sea air and sweetness of this moment, knowing there will be fewer experiences like this as you grow older. Exhaling, I open my eyes as the sun disappears behind the horizon. Slowly, I realize the girlish chatter I hear is not ours but that of other beachgoers packing up at day's end. I realize you aren't here; you never were.

Oh, how I miss you so. There is always room for you when we take family photos. How tall would you be now? What would the chemistry be like with you here in the mix . . . loving, laughing, and playing? I wish I knew, and one day I will. I love you, sweet one.

Our baby would be thirteen today. Officially a teenager, and there would be so much drama in our home with the teenage vibes. Such a beautiful, messy treasure. In her absence lies an unspoken void, fervent longing, and deep melancholy.

But in the emptiness there is a grace that is a beautiful treasure too. I wish I could plan the rite of passage to celebrate her leaving childhood and becoming a woman. I would share the wisdom I have learned over the years, relish the moments of teenage angst, and simply watch her flourish. Instead, the knowledge of who she is now in glory helps me leave behind the self-importance of who I think I *should* be and return to the simplicity and wonderment of embracing where I'm going.

This journey isn't just about navigating loss and grief, it is about the light and peace that come from embracing the role of motherhood in a different sense. It's about rediscovering oneself through the heartache of infertility and how being a mother in the nonphysical sense is an essence that reverberates through every fiber of my being.

Embracing the experience of miscarriage is not easy, and I remained silent for years about my internal struggle. I often thought that if I had gone for help sooner, when the spotting first started, perhaps my girl would have made it. Sitting in the ultrasound room, looking at a dark screen with an empty sac, I became flooded with guilt. The measurement confirmed that my pregnancy had stopped growing at two weeks and four days, yet I should have been six weeks along.

Shame and grief plagued me instantly, and they were feelings I wouldn't shake for years. I blamed myself, yet I hardly knew why. Having a scan when the spotting first started wouldn't have saved the pregnancy. But because I felt like I should have taken action and didn't, I blamed myself. I hid the feelings of anger, grief, and helplessness that come with losing a baby. I didn't give voice to those emotions for a long time, and it remained an unspoken topic even with my husband. We kept tiptoeing around it, not wanting to set each other off or say the wrong thing. We just weren't ever able to put into words what we each experienced and felt. When I see pictures of myself from those few weeks when I was pregnant yet not yet knowing something had gone terribly wrong, I cringe. When I see pictures of myself in the weeks after the miscarriage, I see a woman whose eyes look clouded and distant but with only a hint of the despair that had consumed me.

To this day I still struggle with unanswered questions and the feeling of missing a part of my heart and soul. The thought of "what could be, what should be"' crosses my mind at every holiday and anniversary, during conversations about pregnancy and babies, and when witnessing a stroller being pushed by a mom smiling at her baby or seeing a toddler learning to walk in the park.

This struggle is why I choose to share my story with you. It is why I will continue to raise awareness that motherhood is an essence, an essence that cannot be ripped from us even when things don't go as planned.

My years of silence do not imply that I had nothing to say or that I was afraid to speak up. I had turned inward, and I navigated my grief through moments of silent retreat, meditation, and contemplation to synthesize ideas and reflect. During those years, I learned that mothering extends beyond the societal definition and embraces wisdom, intuitive instincts, cherishment, and fostering growth.

A large part of my journey was acknowledging the misconception I held surrounding shame and miscarriage. Women are often discouraged from sharing their experience of loss, which can lead to feeling isolated and disconnected from their partners, family members, and friends. These women then feel trapped within their own prisons of grief.

However, some women will bravely share their stories, opening a door for others as they each speak their truth. I have learned to gently inquire about those suffering by asking, "How are you doing?" When they are ready to share, I am here to listen with openness in heart, mind, and soul, which will hopefully allow their grief to become a little lighter.

An invitation to share our pain together is one of the first steps toward healing.

Moving forward, I encourage you to reach out, and to not be afraid to hold space for another woman suffering from infertility or miscarriage. Let her know that when she is ready, you will be brave enough to create a safe cocoon where she can come undone and feel the full spectrum of every emotion that surfaces.

Confused about what to say to someone who has had a miscarriage?

"I'm deeply sorry for your loss."
"I'm here for you at any time."
"If you'd like to share your story or feelings with me, I'd love to listen."
"Healing is not linear; take all the time you need."

What NOT to say after someone has a miscarriage:

"It wasn't meant to be."
"Do you think you did something that brought about this loss?"
"At least you know you can get pregnant."
"At least you have a thriving career."

At least, at least, at least. Let's agree to be done with "at least." It is not a compassionate way to start a sentence. Meet grief with nuance, wonderment, and tenderness. Allow your body to ebb and flow as the emotions move through you.

On self-worth, fertility, and #womensupportingwomen

You are a woman. You are powerful. You are worthy. Period. End of story.
Not when you become pregnant . . .
Not when you have your first kid . . .
Not when you have 2.5 kids or more . . .
Not when you lose weight . . .
Not when you do things on a timeline . . .
Not when you [insert your personal comparison trap] . . .

I want women to know that their worth isn't determined by their fertility, and it's healthy to talk about the struggle or moments of jealousy, pangs of regret, and the ongoing waves of grief that arise unexpectedly. I avoided baby showers for close to ten years. I supported expecting friends and family members from afar with gifts and my love sent. It was avoidance at its best, notorious for damaging friendships along the way.

Admittedly, I have judged other women for not sharing their grief or being open to talking about miscarriage. Today, with social media at our fingertips, the access to grief and vulnerability is available within seconds. Everyone has an opinion—some are compassionate, and some are callous and too cruel to repeat.

As women, we don't have to be each other's worst enemies. We can rise together. We can succeed together. We can teach each other that there is a better way to love, and we can create a sense of integrity that we're proud of. We don't need to be waiting and watching for the next woman to fall. We don't need to tear her down and then be relieved when we discover that she is only human too.

We need to champion each other. We need to raise up each other's arms after pain, failure, or exhaustion. We need to say, "It's okay. I see you," because we would never want someone to call our little girl what we are calling each other.

No matter what today is like for you—a day filled with joy, grief, or something in between—I hope you know that you are free to take this moment to breathe. Come back to your body.

If you are excited and motivated to keep giving all your energy to this day, then let this momentary breath energize you. If you are feeling the need to rest and process, let the moment remind you that no matter the outside pressure, you are free to breathe. You are free to take the time to process and rest—it is part of healing.

Practicing self-care is one way you can take back your power. I have learned to listen to my mind, body, and soul over the years. I understand the rhythms of my menstrual cycle, and I have removed the shame associated with it. I listen to my body and provide it with the nutrients, rest, pleasure, and challenges it desires.

I realized that I saw myself as a mother for a long time until I couldn't be one, then everything changed. By gaining wisdom these past years and listening to my mind and soul, I felt the need to create a bolder invitation for this sacred lifeforce we call "motherhood."

My deepest desire for the women who experience infertility is this: Know there is room to grow, even when it does not happen how you envisioned. Some may think you need a viable pregnancy before you can refer to yourself as a mother. But sometimes, we need to do things in an order that makes sense to us. We can embody that mother archetype and essence by nurturing and nourishing ourselves and our dreams like we would with our child. Take that leap of faith. Sharing this vulnerable moment is a leap of faith for me, an action that holds within it a lot of hope, love, and grace. Opening up about loss and candidly expressing grief can create a sense of community and connectedness during an otherwise isolating time. It may also inspire others to do the same.

So, allow yourself the chance to slow down. Learn to replenish your own energies and needs as you heal. Replenish your energy by spending time outdoors, journaling, and learning to be with yourself.

You are no less a womxn if you don't have a child.

I understand the overthinking and sleepless nights spent hoping, waiting, and wishing that someone out there would give you a light. There aren't many people who understand the way your heart beats or know the stories behind your scars. I know that you sometimes feel alone.

Just be gentle with yourself, Mama. You are allowed to be sad, tender at times. You are human. No one expects you to be full of bright happiness all the time. Many things will get a little heavier within you before they get better. But I know for a fact that all of what you are feeling will pass, and in time, you will wake, the dull ache lifting and fading. You will be reminded that your heart is strong and that you are capable of weathering storms.

I know sometimes the world feels like too much for those with hearts like yours, that you feel let down, and that some people have not been kind to you during this time. I need you to understand that whatever occurred was not your fault. You are not a reflection of those who cannot love you, respect you, or show up for you. They are not for you.

You have to find the things in life that bring you moments of peace, be it your favorite song, the midnight sky, the art you create, that walk you crave, a cup of coffee in the morning, your mother's voice, or a playlist that makes your body move. You get to choose what heals you. Hold onto whatever makes you feel alive.

Hold onto what brings you hope. I do.
Because I'm learning to love myself, while finding myself at the same time.

chapter 12

DESIGNED TO OVERCOME: WHEN LIFE GIVES US LEMONS + BREADCRUMBS

MELISSA PUNAMBOLAM

"I call it walking into my worth—an intrinsic worth, value, and human design I would never have uncovered had I not been born into a childhood most might wish they could forget."

IG: @YOURLIFEDESIGNER
FB: MEL PUNAMBOLAM

MELISSA PUNAMBOLAM

Melissa Punambolam is a woman of many titles, hats, and passions, all of which she pours herself into completely. Some of her most admirable titles are Life Designer, Work-Life Balance Expert, Human Connector, and Retreat Host. However, her greatest pride lies in two things: striving to be an amazing single mom to her super-smart, high-energy, and joyful daughter, as well as her innate ability to bring women from all backgrounds together in memorable, cup-filling ways. Although her educational background is an impressive list proving she is proficient in the art of "caring for others," she is also pretty hilarious. If sarcastic quips and witty comebacks were a marketable skill, she'd be a millionaire . . . but she'd still keep doing what she's doing because it feeds her soul. The way to Melissa's heart is simple: buy her food, make her food, or, well, be food—preferably a delectable curry followed by a tea or latte while spending time by the lake. Melissa's life mission is to remove glass ceilings and to not just support but to lift up women who struggle to see their worth, talents, and inherent incredible selves. She is creating a life and legacy that her daughter and future generations will be proud of, and she is loving the path she's taking to get there.

To my daughter, Imani: Thank you for choosing me to be your momma. May you see yourself as I see you—whole, worthy, and divinely badass. I love you with my entire heart and soul.

"W'en rain ah fall ah roof, yuh put barrel fuh ketch am."

~ Guyanese Proverb

(Meaning: There is opportunity for everyone; we must try to grasp it.)

Protector. Advocate. Breaker of Silence.

I never took pride in these traits. In fact, I wanted to give them all away. I mean, a child has a right to be a child, am I right?! Not me. At the time, it felt like those divine rights were stripped away from me and my sole purpose on this planet was to make up for all the wrong my soul had done in past lifetimes. A home filled with turmoil—where walking on eggshells was the norm. Where violence, fear, and poverty could only be explained in one way: punishment for being born. That's why I was undeserving of innocence, laughter, and play, right? What other explanation could there be? Ah, yes, the good ol' *"God chose us to suffer so that we could show others what strength looks like."*

The way I saw it, in this life, I had to protect my caregiver and display insurmountable courage to survive or otherwise I was nothing.

I still praised God, gave thanks, walked to church every Sunday as a teenager with my younger brother in tow, not because I was afraid of being punished further, but because I wanted to show gratitude for my strength, perseverance, and bravery. After all, God chose me to watch countless acts of violence, of varying types and degrees. My job was to see it, call the police, hoping and praying charges would be laid—they never were. Until one day, the system heard one final plea. The unthinkable happened. I was confided in and given full liberty to make the call, exercise my power, my agency. What a massive decision to weigh in on as a child. In hindsight, it was a remarkable day of stepping into my leadership. At the time, though, it felt like my heart, which was already quilted together with dumpster rags since birth, had the patch of intrinsic worth and love torn away from it.

We can all agree that children are especially resilient and brave. They just are who they are designed to be. A tiny, yet unshakable thread flows through them, guiding them intrinsically through their life experiences. Yet all the world tries to shame them, dim their light and power, shun them for simply being who they are and who they are meant to be. They are often forced to play into a box they aren't destined or designed to fit into. And somehow, if you are someone who has managed to break free from these societal norms and shackles, marching to the beat of your own heart, living your truth as you continue to grow older, it is deemed as "pure luck" or, better yet, "coincidence." I don't believe in luck. At all. I believe in divine connection with a straight-up inner knowing. After all, we are designed as humans with this inner knowing; in other words, we are built to know. Let me explain.

After dialing 911, I could feel the inner conflict brewing inside my small, big-eyed, long-haired, unibrowed, volcanically angry body— fear and courage, secrecy and crying out for help, despair and hope. One morning, however, I felt the urge and ping for something new, something different . . . it was a feeling of curiosity that seemed to emerge. Like a seed peeking up from the ground, this feeling nudged until I answered its call for exploration. I felt the urgency to explore these feelings. I couldn't shake it off, even if I tried. Looking back, I realize this is how I was, and still am, designed to live out my human experience, in my own unique way. And truth is, we are all equipped with our own inner roadmap designed to help us have our own human experience. Beneath that nudge for exploration, there was also a small voice within. It was subtle, yet apparent enough for me to take notice, prompting me to wonder:

Will I be okay?
What if life doesn't have to suck?

Little did I realize just how much one single act—following my curiosity and allowing its nudges to guide me—would change my life. It led me to follow the breadcrumbs of my life, ultimately bringing me home to myself.

And so, the journey to rewriting my life script began, following an intuitive life map I was to call my own. The first step was seeking answers.

During one of my spare periods (meaning no class to attend, hence the term "spare") in high school, I found an available computer, used the mouse to find the internet search bar, and with the loud clacking of keyboard keys, I typed "guidance counseling for messed-up angry teenagers." I clicked Enter. In that moment I realized that no one knew what I had been witnessing every single day since the age of five, and finally, at the age of fourteen, I was done. Done being a protector. Done being on the lookout or staying up late, waiting to go to sleep only once it was eerily quiet deep into the night. I was tired from being on constant alert. I was done being responsible; I just wanted to be a silly teenager doing silly things like trying drinks at parties with names like "broken-down golf cart" that could have only been invented by a silly, drunk teenager. To be honest, being a teenager partying my face off at high school parties would have been the faintest shred of innocence I could have had in contrast to the life I led behind closed doors and my strong exterior.

You see, that online search revealed a few counseling agencies. I chose one, and without anyone in my family knowing, I woke at 6:00 in the morning and took a long bus ride to my appointment. I was greeted by a middle-aged woman with a warm smile. She asked why I was there (as any good therapist would), and I, with a confident yet mousy voice, blurted out, "If I don't tell you everything that I've seen and heard, I'm going to grow up really messed up. I don't want to be messed up." After nearly two hours and me not caring that I was epically late for school, that woman shared how impressed she was that a young girl would be so motivated to ask for help. Despite breaking every rule bestowed upon me as a brown-skinned, Canadian-born, Indo-Caribbean female, it felt damn good. No, no, no—not the fact that she was impressed by me—rather, the fact that I broke the rules imposed on me by culture and society and followed my very design of letting others know what I needed. I allowed the world to show up for me. Life had conditioned me to be "normal," to do what everyone else does their way—conditioning that rarely felt comfortable. For the first time ever, in this first true human experience of many, I felt what was natural: that I was worthy of **love, support, and being seen.**

Although the therapist listened with such patience, she needed my mother's permission to have me attend therapy, something I refused to ask for. Just because I broke all the family, gender, and cultural rules didn't mean I was going to reveal that to anyone. Come on! She handed me a cassette tape and told me that no matter what happened, I needed to listen to it every night as I went to sleep. I was to write out any phrases I liked and place them somewhere I could see them. I had the option of rising above it all, she claimed. I didn't consider myself all that wise at the age of fourteen, and at the time I couldn't quite understand what the bleep she was saying. I do know that she wanted me to deconstruct and rebuild my view of life and to make damn sure my parents' decisions about marriage, acceptable living conditions, and other matters didn't determine my trajectory.

In hindsight, taking that **one step** unveiled to me that those inner pings, otherwise known as inner knowing or even inner wisdom, deserve way more credit than we give them. It is how we feel right from wrong rather than being *told* what each one should be. It is how a thought makes sense to the mind (such as *I can't leave home because I need my parents to keep me safe*), but the barometer, which screams hot or cold when something or someone is off base, consistently brings you the truth (such as *they gave me life, but it is no longer safe to be around*). Let's be honest, though. Reconciling between our inner barometer and brain is far from simple, especially at a young age.

The more I reconciled the difference between my logic and my inner knowing, the more I realized how deeply we are all conditioned to depend on logic, which often meant playing Whac-A-Mole with our intuition, all so we can pop up and dodge the ever-present societal smackdown disguised as "expectations" and "norms." Ask anyone who knew me back then: I was socially unpopular, a damn good cheerleader, an academic force to be reckoned with, and a resistor of norms that didn't make sense to me. If a rule meant control over calm, hell could freeze over and I would not follow.

But I digress. You know that tape the therapist gave me? Today, we call a recording of phrases like that "Affirmations," and as you can imagine, the industry of personal development has evolved greatly since my introduction to it all in the mid '90s. But unlike how it is taught and used now, that kind-hearted, white-haired therapist did something we often bypass these days: She guided me on how to reparent myself. Make no mistake—that counseling session was not the be-all and end-all of my journey, but it sure as heck set me on a path of self-discovery, in all its mistakes, failures, and revelations.

I'm proud to declare that I eased up on the rebellion against social (ab)norms . . . almost. I know. I know you were cheering me on; I can feel it! So, let me keep your cheers from turning into blunder. Yes, I attended university away from home and ended up with three degrees, one of which is a master's degree. I was the first cheerleader in Ontario, Canada, to get a scholarship for excellent athletics, academics, and being an awesomely kind human being. I even held two jobs throughout university because I had a lifestyle to maintain—that poor student thing wasn't quite my vibe! It all looked like a fairly normal path until I was getting ready to apply for law school when . . . you probably figured it out by now . . . that ping returned. Being a lawyer was not my thing, much to everyone's disappointment. Don't get me wrong, I can argue with the best of them, but my inner barometer was causing me to question whether there was another way to bring out my inner badass, and this is where it all gets confusing, even for me at times. I studied and trained in social work, which, as you may have heard, is not necessarily equated with badass or even income-growth potential. But where the inner ping goes, I go. When I decided to go one step further by getting my master's degree in social work, that ping moved me to specialize in policy, organizations, and program development.

And there again, that **one step** ended up being the key to doors opening for me, and even more fascinating is how much it opened the door to my human potential.

I need you to know that I have fallen on my face many times, both literally and figuratively. In fact, shortly after I turned thirty years old, my family doctor ordered a brain scan, finding damage I had no idea was even present. I quickly lost trust in the very body that guided me up to that point. I lost trust with every neurological episode I experienced—I lost feeling in my hands, my feet, and all the way up to my face, each instance forcing me to the ground. With every headache and migraine that left me hating the light, I felt like my brain and body were turning on me. Only maybe they weren't. Stay with me here . . . my theory gets better.

I don't know if you get this sense, but I think it's about time I make a confession: It can take a while for me to understand life's signs and signposts. I make this claim because I would find myself caught in cycles that felt more like cyclones. In my career, I would stay in positions overseen by harassing, discriminatory managers for the sake of loving the work and role. I would date what I like to call "yahoos," from addicts to serial cheaters, all for the sake of showing them that I was worth changing for. Oh yeah, folks, that was me alright! Maybe "slow learner" isn't the descriptor after all. Maybe "head-in-the-cloud-of-BS" is the better term. Either way, I had strayed from that one thing, that **one step**—my inner knowing—that never let me stray. Because while I believe that stress is inevitable, martyrdom is not, nor is dancing in a circle that is broken or, better yet, a circle that breaks you. The way I saw it and continue to see it is that sometimes our mind-body is a form of communication, telling us that misalignment exists in our lives (aka illness, malaise, imbalance, burnout, etc.) You get my point. Our job is to stop and reflect, with brute self-honesty, about which areas of our life are out of sync and what we intend on doing to remedy that imbalance. It's like this: We can continue running on the hamster wheel, spinning for as long as we allow it. Many of us will feel like we have no power to stop the spinning, relying on the wheel to stop. But we hold the power—all we have to do is step out of the wheel. Let's agree life is better beyond the mindless spinning on the hamster wheel, yes?

Fast-forward a few years from the discovery of my neurological complications and ongoing medical exploration. I dated and got married. Nice guy, but our marriage didn't last very long. If it weren't for that life phase of discovering my human design and experience, I would not have relearned what I unveiled many years before: I was **worthy of love, support, and being seen. As I am. Unapologetically.** Within the time of our marriage, I became a mother, and it is the most honorable identity and role I have ever had and will ever have, hands down. Once upon a time, in young adulthood, I convinced myself that I was not maternal, that I didn't deserve motherhood, and that I would suck at it. I told myself that I would only cause cycles of trauma to be repeated, and that I would mess up the future generation. I was *so* wrong. I was born to be a co-creating mother, one who lives on purpose and by design, using the one thing no one can ever take away from me: inner knowing, pings, nudges. Fancy names are not required here. I can tell you that I have been mistreated for being *me*. I can tell you that I have been shunned. I can tell you that it has hurt me so much that I have become sick, sad, and silenced. But what picks me up every time is—you betcha!—the pings to get up and show up authentically: for myself, for my daughter, and for others who struggle with owning their intuition.

My childhood was, as one therapist described, like living in a war zone in my own family home. The only detail to add is the fact that I do not fight battles with people and situations. That is not how I am built. I live my truth, and I even tell it like it is. The true opportunity is not found in battle but in feeling, listening, and trusting the inner knowing. I want you to know that this opportunity exists in you too. I believe you have listened before this moment, and I believe even more that you have contemplated taking the **one step**: action. After all is said and done, I am built to notice nudges and to pause, reflect, and follow through on my decisions to act, even if it means culling what is no longer aligned. I believe we all are. Some might call it "running when the going gets tough." I call it **walking into my worth**—an intrinsic worth, value, and human design I would never have uncovered had I not been born into a childhood most might wish they could forget. Paying attention to pings literally saved the trajectory of my life, and shifting **one step** at a time has allowed me to go the distance. Believe it or not I don't have a crystal ball, yet I know I'm just getting started. And I hope as you read these words, you are too. Follow those nudges; follow those ping-filled responses. Tune into your intuitive barometer and allow yourself to be led home to yourself. You have arrived, and you are worthy of being seen, supported, and loved in all your seasons, come what may.

chapter 13

BEING THE LIGHT IN YOUR STORM

GINA BRIGANDI

"Within me lies an indomitable fire that will not be quelled."

IG: @GINA_B3
FB: GINA MARIE

GINA BRIGANDI

Gina Brigandi is a published author, serial entrepreneur, physical therapist, and single mom of three incredible children. Despite the many challenges she has encountered (and is still in the midst of), Gina is at her happiest and is thriving in all areas of her life. A strong advocate for all those who wish to end toxic relationships and break generational patterns, Gina is on a mission to inspire and empower everyone around her to live a wholesome life that brings them joy.

To ... God. My kids who give me the strength to be the strong mama I am today. My dad. My sweet angel, my best friend. Losing you opened my eyes to a different world. My mom. You are my rock and my greatest support system. I don't know what I would do without you.

> *"Sometimes, in life, your situation will keep
> repeating itself until you learn the lesson."*
> *~ Brigitte Nicola*

The infidelity started early on. I had women telling me he was being unfaithful, friends who had suspicions, and then there were those strong gut feelings that most women have—the ones that make you sick to your stomach.

I wanted proof. I was afraid to end my marriage and break up my home without proof. But every time I asked him where he was and who he was with, there was always some kind of "alibi." Soon after asking, the gaslighting would begin. He would give me a-million-and-one suggestions for how I "should" live my life, tell me to distance myself from anyone trying to break up our marriage, and inform me about who I could and could not trust. Every so often there were flowers in the emotional landmines, one in every color and filled with the nectar of sweet nothings, and for a moment, it felt like all was right in our world. The emotional landmines were quelled with promises and sweet talk, only for me to face unfaithfulness all over again. Like a vicious cycle, this routine went on for years. I felt like a single mom. I worked, took care of the kids, and lay awake at night alone wondering who he was with. Therapists, marriage counselors, and others counseled me to leave him. I even lost my best friend in this time. She tried to tell me that he was cheating, but I didn't want to believe it. Thus, our friendship ended, and I was devastated. I possibly lost more sleep over the end of our friendship than the ongoing infidelity and conflict in my marriage.

I couldn't leave because I didn't want to "do that to my kids." I told myself that I would stay miserable so my kids didn't have to come from a broken home. But I felt like a terrible mom. I wasn't showing my kids what being a strong woman and a strong mother looked like, one who is loved, respected, and cherished. I wasn't showing them how real love looks between their parents. Every time I tried to leave, I was reeled right back in. I was gaslit, manipulated, and shamed, but I didn't realize any of that until the marriage was over. Somewhere along the way, I lost my voice and sense of self. I started to believe I was making things up in my head. *Why would I argue if I was the "crazy one?" I didn't have any proof, so what was I trying to gain?*

I was miserable for years. I lost family, friends, and my sense of self-worth. Through it all, I fought hard not to fall into a depression, mourned a miscarriage behind closed doors, and spent a lot of time wondering if this was all my life was meant to be. Life wasn't fun anymore; days became boring and repetitive. I felt my sense of purpose fading away, and my energy and zest for life was nonexistent. I was merely functioning. On the outside, I was there. I was me. On the inside, I felt like a shell of the woman I once was—the fiery, bold, sassy, driven woman I knew myself to be. I went to church and wondered what God was doing *for* me. My conversations with God were filled with questions. Many times, I'd ask Him why I even bothered going to church.

My life felt like one big sham: the Pinterest-perfect, amazing-social-media-posts kind of life. Friends and acquaintances called us a "power couple." Little did they know "real" life for us was nowhere near what we projected. I will not sit here and preach that I was anywhere near the "perfect" wife, but I was a good wife—I was faithful, I took care of our children, I worked forty-plus hours a week to contribute to all household and kids' activities, I made time for date nights, and I truly wanted our marriage to work until I realized how disrespected and emotionally distraught I felt.

Ten years into the marriage and three kids later, I got my proof. It was something I had prayed for for years, and something God had been sending me over and over but I hadn't been paying attention to (or had chosen not to pay attention to). I had been blinded by the manipulation. I hadn't wanted to believe that my life was built on a shaky foundation. But once I had the proof I needed, I lifted my veil and came to a space of acceptance and total surrender. I told him not to come home, then drove to the beach and could not get my mind straight for all the hours I was there.

The next day I woke up thinking, "This is it. This is my out. This is what I've been asking for, praying for." It was my time to live, to be free, and oh, did I live. I loved every minute of my newfound freedom.

The next couple of weeks were uncomfortable. Living together was not easy. There were a lot of fights, and one physical altercation led to an arrest—mine—for a scratch on his head. A week later, I was taken out of my own home with a restraining order. It was the darkest but most enlightening day of my life. That's when I saw the true colors of the person I was married to, that day I was removed from my home. He watched everything unfold with a smirk on his face. The cops in town knew him and told me that despite how wrong and disgusting it was, they had no control over the decision. I needed to pack my bags and leave. The system isn't built to protect victims and survivors unless you know your rights and have a solid support system and lawyer that can help you fight your battle.

Once I exited that toxic home, a huge weight left my body, physically, emotionally, and mentally. Love isn't meant to feel like a weight on your shoulders, and it wasn't until I left that I realized how much trauma I had been carrying. I felt a total shift and a sense of peace. It was transformational, and at this point, I realized I had to do whatever I could to keep my shit together. I refused to let the end of my marriage destroy me. I would do everything in my power to start life over as a single mom, for me and my children. I looked forward to a fresh start even though I knew the road ahead would be challenging.

It has been two years since my separation, my rebirth and awakening to my whole life, and my homecoming to myself. When I started on this journey, my goal was to form a masterpiece with my broken parts, none of which would be possible without focusing on the inner practice of self-love and self-care. When you practice self-love and learn to be content on your own, it's a different kind of love that you give to others. It's a stronger, more nurturing kind of love. You show up differently once you've been through trauma and have done your inner-child healing. You see people differently, you look at the world differently, and you love differently. As I like to say, you see with "eyes wide open."

I began wondering what other people were experiencing in their lives. I wondered if couples were happy. I took time to really listen when I asked people, "How are you?" and became a kinder, gentler soul. I learned to tap into my intuition and listen to my emotions. I learned to tune into my trauma responses and to sit with the feelings that surfaced. I started to honor my desires more and cultivated deeper self-trust. Bit by bit, I healed myself inside out. I attended workshops, sought out therapy, and invested in mentors and coaches to help me further strengthen my mindset while leaning into my emotions. But I don't think I would have been this strong or put in the work if it wasn't for my children. I am obsessed with them. My love for them is strong, and my heart broke for them when I knew my divorce was real. Telling them that their parents would no longer be together was not easy.

I wanted my kids to see a strong and confident mom—a mom who would not give up fighting for what she felt strongly in her heart was right and what she felt she deserved. I came to realize that I deserve a happy, thriving life filled with soul-fulfilling love and an equal part-nership of mind, body, and soul because I am worthy of it, and all people should feel that way. I wanted to teach my boys that they need to respect women while receiving respect back. I wanted my daughter to know that she deserves to be treated like a queen and to treat her man like a king. These are goals I continue to work on with them. I have set boundaries for myself in friendships and with family members, and I will teach my kids how to set them as well.

I knew I needed to do everything I could to break generational traits that bleed down from one generation to the next, and that begins with my own inner healing. I want my kids to be kind, respectful, caring, loyal, and helpful. I want them to learn how to communicate for their wants and needs in their relationships, which is why I have an open table conversation about everything. You name it, we talk about it, from STIs, to oral sex, to drugs, to drinking and beyond. I don't know how my ex parents them, and that isn't my responsibility. My responsibility is to be there for them fully so when they are with me, they are getting a mom and dad in one. I am not perfect, nor do I try to be, and I own up to all my mistakes. My kids call me out when I am not living with integrity, and I have never once tried to hide anything from them. Just as I have learned from all my mistakes, my biggest being staying too long in a toxic relationship, they, too, will learn from my mistakes as well as their own. It is not easy to co-parent. We barely communicate. But I have learned to set boundaries, and I cut him off from texting or calling, and we only communicate very minimally through email. I refuse to be around anyone or anything toxic, so the least amount of communication is better to decrease triggers.

I have learned that it's okay to leave, it's okay to let go, and that life is too short to be anything but happy. Divorce has not been easy, for me or the kids. It's financially and emotionally draining, but avoiding those things is never a reason to stay in an unhealthy and toxic situation. My children did not see a happy marriage or a loving couple. They saw fighting, sadness, and emotional distrust. Kids are resilient. They got used to the back and forth between two homes very quickly, they know they are loved, and they act like fifteen, fourteen, and ten-year-old kids should act. Over the last two years, I slowly became the woman I knew I always was, the woman who was once lost but now is found. If there is any one thing you can take away from my experience, let it be this: Hurt and betrayal don't discriminate, nor is anyone isolated from their effects, and they can happen to the best of us. For me, though this entire experience has been harrowing and painful, it has given me grit and strength and shown me the power of what's possible for a woman determined to rise. What's more, it has shown me that within me lies an indomitable fire that will not be quelled. Trust that voice within that whispers when something doesn't feel right. Lean into your instincts, your truth, and stand in it wholeheartedly. It is true that God will never give you more than you can handle, and sometimes, we are given our exact experiences so we can return home to ourselves, so we can transmute the pain to purpose and be that beacon of strength and hope for all those who need it, and so we can move courageously, despite the fear, one foot in front of the other, in faith that our voices matter, we matter. We will never let anyone take that away from us.

chapter 14

THE EVOLUTION OF A WOMAN

CASIE SCOREY

"At the end
of the day,
time is its own
currency and is
a nonrenewable
resource that is
far more valuable
than money ever
could be."

CASIE SCOREY

Casie Scorey is a former corporate manager turned mom-of-three and household CEO, wife to the man of her dreams, dog mama, life pivoter, joy seeker, silver-lining finder, and a woman who journeys through life by changing direction toward wherever her heart leads her. After becoming a first-time mom, she felt the heartache many moms do when leaving their baby to go back to work, thus missing out on so much precious time together. When Casie realized the struggles and pressures to fit a mold created by society, peers, and herself weren't matching what was in her heart, she made a change that would challenge the beliefs she always held—a change that has brought her a newfound joy and happiness she never imagined.

Dad, thank you for always cheering me on and for all the love you give.

David, you are my rock, my biggest support, my voice of reason, and the love of my life. Thank you for bringing our three incredible children into this world with me and for working hard to support and love your family.

Ava, Sophia, and Jack, words can never express how much you've made an impact on my life, showing me what matters and for proving that love is absolutely infinite.

"Don't think too much, you'll think your whole life away. Just stop, close your eyes, and follow your heart. I guarantee you, it knows the way."

~ Anonymous

Ever since I was little, my dad challenged and encouraged me to work hard and be independent. His work ethic always impressed me and showed me that if you are a hard worker, you can have a good and stable financial life. My dad began his career at age seventeen, had three kids not long after turning twenty, and still managed to work hard enough to get to the top in his company, eventually retiring at fifty-eight. His career path demonstrated his responsibility and level-headedness, and he has a solid retirement and multiple properties to show for it. He set a good example for his kids.

After I graduated high school, I believe my dad, like most caring parents, wanted a similar path for me—to find a solid career where I could plant my roots. However, like many young adults just venturing out into the world on their own, I wasn't sure what I wanted. At that age, there's so much pressure coming from all directions to have life figured out as soon as possible. And while some people have their life plan figured out early on, like my big brother did, most of us have little or no clue how we want our life to look. In hindsight, I know that's normal, and it's okay. But at the time it feels daunting and unsettling. Now that I can look back, I've realized that young adults are really not so different from those older adults who are also, in many cases, still trying to figure out what they want to do with their life as they shift and pivot about, looking for what fits and experiencing what doesn't. The ultimate goal is to follow your heart and find what truly lights you on fire and fills your heart with joy and fulfillment. But often, people are programmed to think that this fulfillment comes from their career. Think about it: What's one of the first questions people ask when having a conversation with someone they've just met? "What do you do?" Everything revolves so much around what we do for a living, the titles we hold professionally, and the companies where we work that it often feels like it is the ultimate factor in defining who we are as a person. But is it?

Truth 1: You are not defined by what you do for a living.

A lot of us are a little lost and confused when we first hit adulthood, and I was no exception. At nineteen, I thought I was in love. I moved in with my boyfriend almost immediately, then made the bright decision to drop out of college to focus more on him. This boyfriend turned out to be a bit of a bad boy, and, well, he wanted to be the bad boy for several girls at once. So, fed up, I met that bad boy outside of the barber shop where he was getting his hair cut one afternoon. In a moment of frustration, I blurted out that I was done with him and that I was moving across the country in thirty days. I had no idea how that information came out of my mouth! The idea of moving hadn't occurred to me at all until that very moment. But after I said it, it sounded like a completely wonderful idea! Why not flip my life upside down and shift things in a new direction? What did I have to lose besides an unfaithful boyfriend? So, I did it. Thirty days later I had packed my life into my Pontiac, and off I went. I had no plan, no job, no home, and no direction. Thinking back to that time, I can't even recall being scared. I somehow knew that I'd figure things out, and I trusted myself to do so. And that's part of the beauty of our life BEFORE babies. We aren't as afraid to take blind risks or to pivot in life. After all, if a risk flops, it's easy to adjust our sails when we only have ourselves to worry about!

By the time I was twenty-five, I was living in my third state since leaving home, this time on the west coast because of an amazing career opportunity. At this point in my life, I was taking things quite seriously on a professional level. Being a career-oriented woman fueled me; it made me feel empowered, and it is how I identified myself. Clearly, I was falling into that trap I mentioned earlier. The harder I worked, the better I felt about myself, and my career validated for me that I could be someone and do something to feel proud of—and get paid well at the same time! So, climbing the ladder became a priority. I also wanted to make my dad proud. I wanted to emulate some version of what he had created for himself, and he certainly never held back from telling me how proud he was when I worked hard and reached goals, which added to my desire for success.

I also married the man of my dreams. To be with me, my husband moved to a country where he knew no one, where he had to learn a new culture and adjust to a completely different environment. During this time, he stayed local, working and caring for our dog, while I really enjoyed my job, traveling a lot both within the states and internationally. Things were smooth, and I was happy, but I wanted us to be closer to family. So, we made the decision to move to my home state where I would start a new career path. I was so excited to tell my family that after years of being across the country, I was coming back home! My love language is quality time, and I wanted more of that in my life with the ones I love the most. We moved into a house in the city about an hour from my family, but I figured we would make time to see them as much as possible. My desire to be successful in my career went to a whole new level, however, and it quickly eclipsed family time with loved ones. Within a month of moving back home, I was working so much that I didn't see my family or my husband. I began working seventy to ninety hours every week, and my husband was alone. Because we were a newly married couple, I wanted to help us get ahead, so I made my career a top priority and ran with it. I had nothing but the best of intentions, but I didn't realize the consequences of putting money before loved ones. My husband became depressed during this time (for the first time in his life), and I didn't know. I was so focused on becoming financially successful that I failed to notice my husband struggling in a country foreign to him, by himself. At the same time, he never complained. He saw I was happy and knew why I was working so hard, and all he wanted to do was be supportive of my goals.

Thinking back on that time brings me to tears. I missed a lot, and I feel it was selfish. I wasn't there where and when I was needed. Thank God my husband is, to this day, an incredibly patient and supportive man. I also didn't see much of my family, which defeated the purpose of moving back across the country in the first place, really. As I write these words, it feels cathartic to release them. Truthfully, until this moment, I've never really fully allowed myself to return to that time in my heart and mind because I have been afraid to feel the pain and regret over making my career the most important aspect of my life when there were more important things that desired my attention. I'll never get that time back to change it. But I can learn a lesson from it, and I have. And that lesson became the most wonderfully useful gift when I welcomed my first child into the world.

Truth 2: You can get lost along the way, and that's okay, as long as you learn from it.

When I had my first child, something immediately changed deep within me. My world changed, my heart changed, and the wiring in my brain changed. I no longer felt a connection with my career, and I no longer got satisfaction from it. Instead, I felt empty, lost, and distracted at work. My mind was on my daughter, and my heart ached to be with her. Instead, I was gone nine hours a day while she was in daycare. Her caretakers were great, but instead of me experiencing the days with my daughter, they were the ones telling me what she liked to eat or what new things she was learning to do. They saw her reach milestones that I was missing, and they were getting to know her personality and sharing things with me about her that I didn't know as well as they did. They got to feed her and snuggle her to sleep. And while I was so grateful for these amazing ladies, it left me feeling sad and lost. *I'm her mom. I should be the one with her for these moments.* Instead, a typical day with my daughter involved waking up early, putting her in her baby swing in front of the television so her dad and I could get ready for work, packing her things for the day, getting her dressed, then rushing out the door to drop her off at daycare so we could get to work on time. Nine hours later, I would pick her up from daycare, make dinner, run her bath, get her down to sleep, then wake the next morning and repeat, repeat, repeat.

I realized my desires had evolved just as much as I had with motherhood. While my ambitions and desires for success still burned brightly within me, I realized that my idea of success had evolved. I realized that motherhood, in a way, was my rebirth—my chance to do things in a way that worked for me and my family. And yet again, I was drawn to my love language: quality time. I felt there just had to be a way to make it happen. I could be a woman who was successful, thriving as a mother and partner. I had to give myself permission to evolve and see this possibility, which was something that never would have happened until the birth of my firstborn. And the desire to make this possibility my reality only burned brighter with the birth of each of my children.

Truth 3: With each child you have, you, as a woman, are reborn.

Before I had my children, I used to tell people that I could never be a stay-at-home mom. NO WAY! Not me! I worked too hard in my career to just give that all up. And how would that even work financially? But once I became a mother, everything felt different. With me working all week and my baby in daycare, we had very little time to bond as mother and daughter. Sure, we had the weekends, but my heart truly felt that that time just wasn't enough. And when it came to motherly instincts, I didn't want to ignore what my heart was telling me. I simply couldn't leave her every day anymore; my heart wouldn't let me. But it wasn't easy. I was the breadwinner in our family. How could I even think of prioritizing being with my daughter every day over my career and income when there was a child I was responsible for? Children aren't cheap! But after a discussion with my husband about the possibility of me staying home, I knew we could do it if it was that important. We could adjust our lifestyle and expenses and make sacrifices wherever we could. After all, the sacrifice of giving up a few luxuries in life was nothing compared to the sacrifice I was already making by giving up time with my daughter. There was no comparison. I didn't want to make the same mistake I made in the past by putting career and money first. So, I dusted off the risk-taker side of myself and trusted that things would be okay like they had always been whenever I made major pivots in my life.

Once my daughter was ten months old, and with the support of my husband, I left my career and a solid salary and became a stay-at-home mom to our daughter. Though this decision added extra financial pressure on my husband, he was fully supportive; he, too, wanted our daughter to be raised by me full time. At the end of the day, time is its own currency and is a nonrenewable resource that is far more valuable than money ever could be. We often think that we are chasing financial success, but really, if you take a moment to reflect on it, it is freedom that we are after: the ability to wake up when we want, to be available to our loved ones without having to ask permission from anyone or worry if our livelihood will be affected, to live life on our terms, and to devote our energy to what matters most (something that looks different for each of us). For me, I wanted to be devoted to my daughter, to build a bond with her. Perhaps, subconsciously, I wanted to make amends with my own soul for the time I spent prioritizing my career and the golden handcuffs over quality time. I no longer wanted to put my love language on the back burner. I wanted to live it, breathe it, and be it.

So, I stayed home with Ava, not missing a single thing: I took her to the park and the zoo, on playdates, and to the coffeehouse. We went shopping, to museums, and on walks. We visited friends and family, snuggled in bed in the mornings while watching cartoons, ate breakfast together every single day, and made Play-Doh and paper snakes.

I laughed and enjoyed life with my most precious gift from God, my daughter. We moved to a less expensive house, stopped going to restaurants as much, and found other areas to cut back on financially that we wouldn't even really miss in order to continue to make this life change possible.

Truth 4: You're always going to make sacrifices, so you just have to choose which things in life are most worth sacrificing for.

It's now been seven years since I left my career to be a stay-at-home mom for my daughter. Since then, we have welcomed two more beautiful children into our family. As a homeschooling mom of three kids, I find immense joy in being the one to raise them and teach them about life. I have never found more joy or love in anything like I do in my kids. I wouldn't want to be doing anything at this time in my life other than being right where I am with them. And though I can say that I don't need external validation about my choices in life, I know with certainty in my heart that my dad is far prouder of me today as a mom than he was of me as a career woman. And there is no better compliment to me than that.

chapter 15

BOUNDLESS BEAUTY

NATHALIE AMLANI

"I am most in alignment when I believe in myself, when I trust my intuition and instinct, when my mindset is in a place of abundance and boundless beauty, and when I affirm love of self."

NATHALIE AMLANI

Nathalie Amlani is the founder of Pictonat Creative, where she helps women entrepreneurs ignite their brand online with creative storytelling, brand photography, and online strategy. In her five years at Pictonat Creative, Nathalie has launched a podcast, has become a motivational thought leader, and has helped more than thirty women entrepreneurs grow their business with her intuitive approach to visual storytelling. Prior to entering the world of entrepreneurship, Nathalie was a senior project manager in financial services for seventeen years where she managed large-scale technology and operations projects. A graduate from the Rotman School of Management, Nathalie holds a master's degree in business administration with a focus on strategy and marketing. When not hard at work bringing to life her creative ideas, she's an energetic mom of two kids who enjoys exploring new places with her family, playing strategy games, practicing mindfulness, and working out on her Peloton. Nathalie is often described as tenacious, positive, and highly intuitive. She is known to never give up and is passionate about helping others grow and thrive in both business and life, and she believes that everyone has a beautiful story to tell. Tell your story, elevate your brand.

To my partner in crime, my husband, who always believes in me and is there to catch me when I fall and to lift me up—I love you. To my kids who have truly taught me the power of "now" and what it means to live in the moment, who have ignited the passion in me—I love you. To my mom, thank you for always being there for me and for being you—I love you. And to my friends and community that have each sparked a light in me, shining the way for my journey to self: May you be happy and filled with boundless love and success.

"Love yourself as much as you can, and all of life will mirror this back to you."

~ Louise Hay

It felt like my life was frozen in time, replaying on an endless loop, every single day. I was consumed with fatigue, and all I wanted to do was sleep. My mind was foggy, and any ounce of energy I had was used to appear "normal" on the job or in social settings. I went to the doctor for a checkup, had my blood work done, and it all came back normal. I thought to myself, *Maybe I need a vacation; maybe I am overworking myself, trying to scale and grow my business.* So, I took a week off work, packed my bags, and headed up north to a chalet with my husband and kids. I expected to miraculously find bliss, a sense of calm and release, and for the energy to flow back into my body like a waterfall—an awakening. Instead, the naps in the day became more frequent; all I wanted to do was to sleep in a dark room. When I was awake, my mind was foggy. I didn't have enough energy to engage in play with the kids. I felt guilty, frustrated, and most of all, sad. I felt consumed with darkness. At that point, I knew it was time to ask for help, and so I did. A couple weeks later, I was diagnosed with depression.

Three years earlier, I was pregnant with my second child, working at my demanding job at the bank. With more than fifteen years of tenure at the bank, working in the fast-paced environment, I thought it was normal to work myself to the bone, to put in the extra hours, and to be at their beck and call. I thought that was the way it was supposed to be. I was always putting my heart into work and going the extra mile, tying my self-worth to my job. I was always striving to grow my career and climb the ladder it wasn't easy. After my first child was born, I scaled back on my hours, and though they still counted as overtime, it was a reduction nonetheless. I reduced my extracurricular activities at work by volunteering on fewer committees so that I would have enough time to drop off and pick up my son from daycare. The silver lining from reducing my hours? I became more efficient at work, maximizing the little time I had in comparison to before. I was hopeful that I could still grow my career while growing a family. During my second pregnancy, I was more tired, I had extreme nausea, and I was constantly eating plain crackers and chewing ginger candies to try to ease the symptoms. I didn't want to appear "weak." When I did, I received little sympathy. I was working on a high-profile project that had a lot of client-facing time with higher-level executives. I put in extra effort and hours to make up for the hours off for checkups with my obstetrician or having to leave "on time" to pick up my son from daycare, and yet it didn't feel like enough. After I announced my pregnancy, my boss's demeanor toward me was cold and devoid of any empathy, and my coworkers were rude. *What was going on?* I went home in tears more often than not—it was so traumatizing. The familiar feelings of guilt and inner conflict made themselves known yet again. This time around, it was ten times worse. I so badly wanted to make everything work—the growing career and the growing family. Yet, the harder I tried to do so, the more I felt like I was failing. I soon felt totally worthless. Though I was physically present, I felt further away both mentally and emotionally. I no longer recognized the woman I'd become, and I felt like a shell of the woman I once was.

My chase for this utopian ideal of wanting to balance it all perfectly and not have a thing out of place was not something new. No, this was a pattern I recognized well enough. It was how I coped growing up to ensure I reached a particular destination, a goal, so that I'd somehow feel "enough." I grew up in a single-parent household. My mom had me when she was young, and when I was a teenager, people often asked if we were sisters. We are now closer than ever, but growing up, I felt distant from her. I didn't understand why she was always working long hours (to support us) or why she had to study all the time (to get a degree to help support us), and I couldn't relate to what she was going through with trying to adjust to a new country on her own with zero family or support plus learning a new language. In my mind, I felt abandoned. I felt like I was on my own, and I needed to find ways to survive and thrive. Always an observant child, I learned the ropes of life and social norms by watching and learning. I now call it being highly intuitive. I had a carefree childhood and would spend lots of time outside, exploring and playing both by myself and with friends. I craved companionship and associated having companionship with being loved. Being an only child, I experienced feelings of loneliness a lot; it was an empty feeling. To fill the void, I'd engage in activities, explore hobbies, and learn new things. In fact, this desire to learn led me to complete my photography certificate that led to the start of my own business years later! As I grew older, I dreamed of having a degree, a postgraduate degree, a well-paying job, and a family. I mapped out my goals, and for the most part, I stuck to that map—I graduated university with a bachelor's degree in commerce, completed my master's degree in business administration, got certified as a Project Management Professional, gained seventeen years of experience at the bank, and got married and had two kids. It felt like everything was right on track, and right on schedule, just how I envisioned it. I was going for a fairy-tale ending, the ultimate utopian dream. For me, it was all about the destination, not the journey.

When I was diagnosed with depression, it hit me hard. I had accomplished my goals, checking off every list item in my life. I had everything I dreamed of as a child, so why did I feel this sense of sadness and emptiness? I tried to dissect the triggers and the causes to uncover the reason behind it all. *Why me? Why now?* I went through therapy, took antidepressants, and indulged deeper into yoga and meditation. At the same time, I was gaining weight from all the medication and emotional eating. I was already insecure about my postpartum body at this point, so as a solution, I hired a personal trainer. I felt like there had to be a solution to everything. If I checked off the list of things I must do, I would be healed. Of course, I soon learned that it wasn't as simple as that. I wasn't seeing the physical transformation fast enough. Inside, however, I felt strong. My muscles were stronger than before, and my energy levels were finally reaching a healthy balance. I no longer felt the overwhelming exhaustion. But on the outside, it was as if nothing had changed. I still looked the same. I would think to myself, *People will still ask me if I'm pregnant. I will never bounce back. Why isn't it working?* I realized my sense of acceptance and self-worth was tied to my outer appearance.

I continued seeking help; I wanted someone to help me fix myself. I worked with amazing business coaches, therapists, light workers, energy healers, and mindfulness experts, and I engaged in many supportive communities. I attended soul circles that opened my heart in unexpected ways. One of my favorite journal prompts that really got me to dig deep and open my heart was one by mindfulness expert and soul circle facilitator, Ashleigh Frankel: **What do I need today? How will I honor what I need?** Through free-flow journaling the answers to these questions, I was able to connect to my heart and tune into myself.

Tuning into my soul and strengthening my intuition has been and always will be an ongoing practice. The more I paid attention to what I needed, the quicker I was able to move through any challenges. Anytime I lacked clarity, I tuned into my intuition where the answers were clear as day, a "full-body response" as they call it. Each time, I gained strength. My self-worth and my confidence returned. I am now well-versed on how to unblock my energy and use my intuition to help guide me. But this shift didn't take place overnight. It was gradual progression that led to my transformation as I started to shift my mindset and my beliefs. In her book *Badass Habits,* Jen Sincero writes, "Shift your identity to match the habits you're adopting. Changing your actions in order to form a new habit without also changing who you're being is like running into the wind: Yes, it's possible to put your head down, run as hard as you can, and gain some ground, but you're much more likely to give up and return to your old ways than if you run in the same direction as the wind."[1] As I learned to trust myself and understand love and the true meaning of it, I started to lead with an open heart as my authentic self, including embracing my physical postpartum body.

I have realized that I am most in alignment when I believe in myself, when I trust my intuition and instinct, when my mindset is in a place of abundance and boundless beauty, when I make time for myself, and when I affirm love of self. Everyone I met along the way became my community, my supporters, my friends, my colleagues, my network—each a twinkle of light on my journey. I soon learned what it meant to ask for help and that I was never alone or abandoned, and I shed the fear of being judged. I was full of love from within. Though I didn't see it or understand it at the time, in my unraveling to return home to myself, my soul took a different form and was purposeful in leading me to where I am today sharing my story. During this time, my business thrived and grew and entrepreneurship felt completely aligned. In fact, I experienced the most business growth during the time that I was going through my episode of depression and self-realization. It was as if my business was growing and transforming alongside my own transformation. I truly believe that there is a connection between mindset, energy, and business, so much so that I connected with a soulful friend to create a podcast on this very topic.

At the time of each hardship, I felt like it was the end of the world. But it was all meant to happen and unfold just the way it did, as part of my story, my journey, and my life so that I would discover my purpose and cultivate deep self-trust and self-love. My journey helped me:

- Learn the meaning of love—it is not based on my performance at work or my outer appearance, it is love and acceptance of self.
- Learn the truth of living in the moment, the healing that practicing mindfulness provides.
- Realize that everything I need is already inside me.
- Cultivate an attitude of gratitude, and manifest success and abundance in my life.
- Experience the power of mindset.
- Share my story and show others the beauty and joy of life and the lemonade that surrounds us and is within us—it's all about the journey, *not* the destination.

At every moment, we are capable of finding the light within—a light that is fueled by love and passion and an inherent worth and desire so deep that it paves the way for others to do so as well, letting them know they are not alone.

If I had a chance to change anything about my journey, I wouldn't change a thing.

I believe that I am exactly where I'm supposed to be.

I believe that I am worthy.

I believe that we can manifest anything our heart desires.

I believe that there is boundless beauty and joy.

I believe in love, and that I am love.

And so are you.

chapter 16

TOO MUCH

CHIARA FRITZLER

"Your truest self—
the incredible
personality traits
you were born
with—is perfect
and not something
that should
ever require
justification."

CHIARA FRITZLER

Chiara Fritzler is a writer who loves old books, red wine, and Hawkins Cheezies. Her blog, *All of Your Baggage Should Be Carry-On—Stop Feeling Sorry for Yourself and Find Your Joy*, was created to help others realize they aren't defined by their diagnoses, pasts, jobs, or any other titles they may have placed on themselves (or that others have given them). Chiara innately and deeply "feels" her life while she goes through it, and for most of her life, she has felt pressure to suppress her naturally outspoken nature and drive to lead. A forty-something single mom to a toddler, Chiara has navigated polycystic ovarian syndrome, weight issues, anxiety, depression, job loss, infertility, and divorce. Nonetheless, she refuses to give in to the pity of "Why me?" and instead focuses on "What am I meant to do with the place I'm in?"

To the girls with unapologetically full, wild hearts: Refuse to let the world convince you to deny who you were created to be, regardless of the backlash from those envious of your incredible uniqueness. May we remember who we were before the world told us who we should be.

"There were always in me, two women at least, one woman desperate and bewildered, who felt she was drowning and another who would leap into a scene, as upon a stage, conceal her true emotions because they were weaknesses, helplessness, despair, and present to the world only a smile, an eagerness, curiosity, enthusiasm, interest."

- Anaïs Nin

Care too much.

Say too much.

Show too much.

Need too much.

Feel too much.

Want too much.

Strive too much.

Are too much.

Have you ever been made to feel like you're *too much?* Do you feel like you are constantly holding back or like you're pushing against your very nature?

Why do we feel this way?

Take a moment and reflect. Close your eyes and slowly breathe in through your nose and out through your mouth. Okay, you're reading these words, so close your eyes and breathe ten breaths while thinking about any time you were made to feel like you weren't acceptable when you showed up as a genuine version of yourself.

I'll wait.

How did that feel? How many examples did you come up with?

How many times did the same person appear?

Thinking back over my childhood, I believe that I've almost always felt like I'm "too much," like perhaps God missed a step when he created me. I feel like the quiet, demure, deferring, apologetic, smile-and-nod coding that females are apparently supposed to have wasn't installed properly in my brain. Now, I'm not saying that being quiet and demure are traits that can't be wonderful, I'm just saying that they're "typical" female traits that I don't have and haven't ever been able to force upon myself.

As a child, I loved wearing dresses and always wanted to look pretty, but I wanted to play with the boys. I didn't want to sit in circles and play clapping games or dress dolls. I wanted to run, jump, climb, and fall down. And fall down I did. Before I turned ten years old, I had stitches in my head four times, all a result of taking ridiculous risks like jumping on my bed with my eyes closed or standing on a swirly chair at McDonald's.

When I was in grade one, my teacher told me that I wasn't allowed to play with the boys because it wasn't "proper." So, I started spending my lunches and recesses with an older girl who lived two doors down from my family. I was then told that I wasn't allowed to play with her either because I needed friends my own age. (I still harbor a bit of resentment against that teacher, to be honest.) I didn't want to play with the girls in my grade; they were boring. But, as a highly social child, I wanted connection and friends, so I decided to join in . . . okay, not so much join in as announce my status as the supreme leader of grade-one girls. I essentially told the girls in my grade that they were my friends, like it or not. I walked around the schoolyard with my arms outstretched, not allowing anyone to walk in front of me and only permitting my best friends to walk beside me. I'm honestly not sure why I behaved this way; I can only surmise that it may have been one of the first manifestations of my natural leadership skills (also called "being bossy" if you're female), and I used these skills to show my teacher that, in essence, she didn't control my life. This behavior continued until grade three at which time I was very abruptly and unexpectedly taken down a few rungs. But I've already written about that in my blog, so I won't belabor it here.

Throughout my childhood and young adult life, I collected experiences of being made to feel like my natural tendencies weren't tolerable. Junior high was especially tough for me. I was very awkward and extremely uncomfortable in my own skin. Because I was outspoken and wasn't one to put up with being mistreated, teachers often assumed that I was the troublemaker while their backs were turned. A particularly scarring incident was in grade eight when a boy came up behind me on the field and pulled down my pants and underwear, right after the bell rang to come back inside. While I stood in mortification, I flailed toward him, reaching for anything I could get a hold of. I managed to grasp his ear and damn near pulled it right off. Guess who got in more trouble? You betcha, it was me—the feisty girl who refused to roll over and die.

When I think about times I was made to feel like I was "too much," or that my strong personality wasn't acceptable, I also think a lot about my previous career. I spent almost twenty years as an occupational health and safety professional, which meant that most of my time was spent working with or for construction, oil and gas, or manufacturing companies. I'm sure it's not groundbreaking to say that these are fairly male-dominated, masochistic (at worst) and female-tolerant (at best) industries. I am not one to tolerate being treated poorly, nor do I defer to anyone simply because of their title. And I most definitely am not one to allow the women I work with (who aren't so secure in their voices) to be bullied or mistreated.

Allow me to digress slightly—I often think I was meant to live in the times of *Downton Abbey* or *Bridgerton* because of chivalry and how badly I want to wear the beautiful gowns. But let's be honest: A woman with my kind of spirit would not fare well, and I'd tear off my corset in the middle of some proper dance and then be hanged in the main square or something.

Back to mistreatment at work and not in town squares. . . . The most prominent example of being mistreated because of my "too much-ness" is when I worked for a new division of a global organization. They had somehow been granted a very large contract for work they had never done before and had to scramble to get people; I was one of the "scramble" people. The director of my division and I had met through previous work interactions, and he offered me a ridiculous amount of money, a company vehicle, and a four-day work week. I was pretty unhappy with my current job (I had been bullied by an egotistical VP, and I had stood up for myself, God forbid), so I took the position and looked forward to the challenge.

Scrambling to find people to fill positions often means that perhaps the best people don't end up in those roles. My first day on-site, I was met with a misfit group of employees. Some slept in their trucks most of the day, some were lovely and wonderful people, and some were inexcusably arrogant, rude, and self-important blowhards.

There was one particular man at my site who fit the "blowhard" definition, and I'm not exaggerating when I say that it's the kindest description I can grant him. I have thoughts surrounding administrative types of work, so hear me out and keep reading before jumping to conclusions. I believe that administrative work is something that almost anyone can do . . . but very few can truly do well. For those of you who do this work and do it well, I am in absolute awe of you; I can barely run my own life let alone be the friendly face of an organization while staying on top of the needs of everyone who works there. Our administrator at this particular site was incredible. She never slacked off, she was always first to arrive and last to leave, and she oozed both kindness and efficiency. She also happened to be blind in one eye and deaf in one ear, which sure as sugar didn't affect her ability to absolutely kill it at her job. As the only two women on-site, we became quite close friends.

The aforementioned blowhard often picked on my friend. He would speak into her deaf ear intentionally and then berate her for not doing what he asked. He would stand on her blind side and ask why she wasn't looking at him. One time when she hadn't heard his instructions (I use "instructions" intentionally because he never asked for anything, he always instructed or told), he decided to humiliate her. It was a blistering cold day out in the middle of the prairies, and he forced her to stand on the main road (where all site staff, including hundreds of contractors and subcontractors, drove through) and "play out" what he had asked of her, including pretending to drive a car, while he sat in his nice warm truck, shouting his demands at her.

Is your blood boiling? Mine was. Every day. Before this insulting event, I had already filed complaints with HR on her behalf. She had made it very clear to me that she needed the work so didn't want to create waves, and HR told me that they couldn't do anything unless she was the one who filed the complaints. The incident of the forced public humiliation of my friend was the absolute LAST straw for me. I didn't care that the blowhard was much higher up in the food chain than I was. I asked him to come into the back office where I very calmly explained to him that his behavior was not acceptable. I would not tolerate it to continue, and for whatever little amount it was worth, he would hear from me every time he treated my friend poorly.

I won't honor him by saying more about his response to me other than to say that he started it with "Little girl, you stupid, insignificant little girl" (I was thirty-seven at the time), but it's worth mentioning that every day after I spoke to him he not only bullied our administrator more ruthlessly but also tried to pick on me. I say "tried" because I didn't ever let him know that he was getting to me. I had the luxury of being able to leave the office in my company vehicle and drive somewhere on-site, a luxury not afforded to my friend. I filed at least six more complaints with HR, but nothing was done. I was eventually relocated to another site because I (apparently) created too many waves and was "too much of a disturbance." When I quit that job a year later, that man was still employed. I don't know what became of my friend, but I was told she was forbidden to speak with me ever again, unless she wanted to lose her job.

I was fortunate that with all the upset of this career position to have met a wise, kind friend—a safety professional at another site, a man about ten years older than I—who became a close confidant. He's one of those men who isn't intimidated by strong women, who married a strong woman, and who is raising strong daughters. He came up with a phrase that initially might sound sexist, but the premise makes sense: "Put a mustache behind it." His point was that if, as a woman, you want to be taken seriously and to walk away respecting yourself, you must think, "If I were a man, how would I expect to be treated?" He wasn't implying that women *should* ever expect less; he was implying that as women, we are often raised to expect less, want less, or told that what we want is too much; that what we expect or what we think we deserve is so much less than men. He bought me a gift when I left that company—a mug that says, "May you be blessed with the confidence of a mediocre white man."

Why, as women, do we feel apologetic for expecting and asking for what we deserve? I have to tell you, during my years working in male-dominated industries, one of my favorite self-created games was, "What do I need to say to this dude to make him actually think he's smarter than I am and to make him do what I want in the end?" It was like a never-ending sales job but with men as my unknowing customers. I knew I could outwit most of them, so I would learn about them and figure out what I needed to do to get them to participate in whatever I needed done.

While I thoroughly enjoyed this "game" I made up for myself, I do see that it's terribly sad that I didn't feel safe or comfortable enough to simply state the facts and my opinion or provide expert insight. Feeling like it's my job to make a man feel smart by giving him credit for my ideas isn't the message I want to give my daughter, and it's hopefully not the one anyone would give their sons, for that matter.

Years ago, I began a friendship with an older woman who worked at my church. I was instantly drawn to her strength, her wisdom, and her unapologetic nature of providing her astute and clever intuition. I will never forget what she told me one afternoon as we had coffee together: "Chiara, God gave you this inner strength, this ability to speak up, to be seen and heard. He put these personality traits within you, and to deny these gifts and reject them or even apologize for them is discrediting your very nature and the One who created you." Regardless of what your faith or belief system is, these words resound with incredible truth. Your truest self—the incredible personality traits you were born with—is perfect and not something that should ever require justification. I know that it's hard, so hard, to believe that who we are is acceptable and worthy given the constant bombardment from every angle that no part of who we are is actually okay as it is. Sadly, this same woman was "let go" by my church, and I have no doubt that her intelligence and ability to speak her truth was one of the reasons why. Upon telling someone who is well-established in the church about my friendship with this woman, I was told, "Be careful, you don't want to get too close to her, let alone become like her." Oh, but I did.

One of the reasons I want to be like this friend from church is because I'm a mom to a little girl. My daughter is three years old, and her personality is an inspiring balance between outspoken, unapologetic independence, absolute silly hilariousness, and incredibly gentle kindness. She has already been called "too much" and a "drama queen" (something that I have been called on numerous occasions), and I have received much more unsolicited advice on how to parent my "spirited" (as "they" call children like her) daughter than I would ever welcome. But here's the thing: I wouldn't have her any other way. I won't have to worry about her being bullied at school or at work. She already has a keen sense of who she is and what she wants and is joyfully unrepentant about it. I am so incredibly proud to be her mother, and while I occasionally question whether I enjoy being a mom, I can say without a doubt that I love being HER mom. Having her as my daughter means that I, too, need to continue owning my "too-much-ness" so she never holds back or denies who she truly is. And for that, I will work tirelessly so she will believe that she is whole, worthy, incredibly enough as she is and that she is not "too much" at all. All her dreams, desires, wants, and way of being are all just a part of the imperfectly perfect person she is. And who she is, who you are, and who I am is never too much.

chapter 17

WHEN LIFE GIVES YOU LEMONS, PLANT ITS SEEDS AND GROW YOURSELF

STEPHANIE DINSMORE, MSW

" . . . happiness comes from following your heart; a heart that is driven and guided by the passion and wisdom you develop in your journey to grow into being the best version of yourself."

STEPHANIE DINSMORE

Stephanie Dinsmore has many passions and aspirations. She holds a master's degree in social work (MSW) and is passionate about mental health and whole wellness. She is the owner/founder/clinical lead at her private practice, Mindful Path Counselling. In addition to running her private practice, she works at Wilfrid Laurier University as a counselor in the Student Wellness Center. Dedicated to professional development, she is pursuing her doctorate in educational leadership at Capella University. Stephanie resides in Brantford, Ontario, where she is a mom to her beautiful twelve-year-old daughter, Hailey, and her three fur babies, Duke, Diego, and Leonard, and is a wife to her incredible husband, Kyle. Stephanie enjoys CrossFit, meditation, and hiking with friends.

To my daughter, Hailey: You're the reason WHY I am the person I am today. You inspire me. You bring me joy with your love, energy, and excitement for life. To my husband, Kyle: Your love, kindness, and encouragement motivate me to be my best self. I'm so blessed for the life we have created together. To my family and friends (you know who you are): You helped me raise Hailey when I was a single mother and allowed me to pursue my dreams to attend university, not once but four times. I am forever grateful. To all the moms out there who question if they can do it, YOU CAN. I see you; it's not easy.

*"Loving ourselves through the process of owning
our story is the bravest thing we will ever do."*

~ Brené Brown

There have been many times in my life when I've felt as though I've lived multiple lifetimes within this one already, which can be attributed to my own journey as well as to the type of work I do professionally, witnessing people from all walks of life navigate the curveballs that get thrown their way. Students, especially, experience numerous stressors and challenges, as is expected entering their first year of postsecondary school.

For me, taking a year off after high school was both rewarding and challenging as I began to navigate the real world. I was raised Roman Catholic and was taught that sex is reserved for marriage. I was engaged and had convinced myself that it was less of a sin since we were on our way to being married and fully committed to one another. Wow . . . was I wrong. Little did I know that I was in for a cold awakening and that life as I knew it would dramatically change.

The fall before school started, we broke up, and I was left shocked, depressed, and fearful about entering the next chapter of my life alone.

But to my surprise, I was not alone. I was twenty years old, an undergraduate studying leadership (which quickly changed to criminology) at Wilfrid Laurier University, and I was very much pregnant. Convinced that the drugstore tests were inaccurate and that my hormones were off from all the stress I was experiencing, I made an appointment to see a doctor to weed out any uncertainty. Once there, the doctor happily confirmed I was indeed pregnant and scheduled my first ultrasound. I remember leaving the doctor's office stunned, my hands full of pamphlets describing all the possible options I could ultimately choose from. I sat in my car, gripping the steering wheel. Then the shock passed as quickly as it came, and without a doubt in my mind, I knew I would keep this baby and raise him or her on my own.

Sometimes We Make Lemonade

Being a student, I was still living at home with my parents and brother. My parents housed me as their way to support me through my studies since the cost of tuition was outside their means, and I was fearful that my home would be ripped out from beneath me once I disclosed that I was pregnant and planned on keeping the baby and raising him/her alone. The conversation with my parents and brother, who happened to be present, went as well as expected. My mother stared at me in shock, my father said nothing and then left the table, and I just sat there, unsure as to what to do next. I gave everyone time to wrap their minds around what I had shared, and my mother was the first to show support for my decision. My father took some talking to, but once he realized a grandbaby was coming, he was on board.

This pregnancy would prove to be a critical moment in my young adult life. Who I was and who I would become was forever changed.

As I learned to navigate my life as a pregnant student, I learned quite quickly that my experience would be very different than that of my peers. I attended classes after work and spent my time studying and preparing for my baby to arrive. I found a wonderful group of friends with whom I eventually shared my news, friends I am still close with today. I am forever grateful for their love and support along the way. My pregnancy was a breeze; I guess I can thank my youth for that. I worked full time during my first year of studies and was determined to plan as best as I could with the short time that I had. Before I knew it, and eleven days past my due date, Hailey arrived—a beautiful baby girl on September 21, 2008. Soon after, I fell into a depression. I noticed that I was anxious all the time, I had mood swings, I had trouble bonding with my baby, I was fatigued, and I had cognitive problems and negative emotions. I felt like a failure as a mother because I wasn't married to my daughter's father, and my feelings of worthlessness were so powerful that I was unable to function. My parents were concerned, kept pointing out the signs, and encouraged me to see a medical professional. When I met with my doctor and shared my symptoms and my experience, I was diagnosed with postpartum depression. My doctor encouraged me to access mental health counseling at the local hospital, to find ways to bond with my baby, to increase my sleep, and to find time for myself. Though these tasks were not easy for me, I found the courage to ask for help. I waited for a judgmental response when I said the two words that made asking for help a bit easier—"I'm struggling"—but what I got was quite the opposite: love and kindness. I was a kid raising a kid, and in reality, I needed all the help I could get.

A lot changes during your first year of motherhood. Your friendships evolve. Your relationship with your family evolves. You evolve. Before motherhood, asking for help was not something I would do, but it became something I relied on so I could participate in my studies, work, and maintain a social life. I struggled to balance my responsibilities as a parent, be a student, and still have fun like other kids my age, but we developed a pretty good routine that first year. I found comfort in my daughter's energy and excitement for life, and I looked to her for guidance when the pace of our life was moving too quickly or if we couldn't manage. Her happy demeanor and willingness to be with just about anybody allowed me to have the freedom I still desired (and possibly had too much of).

Spring 2009 came around, and I was ready for my first weekend away with my girlfriends. We decided to go camping only a short distance away in case I needed to get home for Hailey. The weekend was full of laughter, campfires, and times to unwind, and it was pivotal for a few reasons: It was the weekend I met my best friend and the weekend I met a guy. He was my first relationship since my daughter's father, and I was hooked. I was so blinded by love that I was oblivious to the fact that our relationship was unhealthy. We dated for just over two years, most of which was fun and exciting but emotionally draining. He often made me choose between time with him and time with my daughter, and my self-esteem was so low that I often chose to be with him. As our relationship progressed through both good and bad times, so, too, did my university years. Soon, I had to choose whether to continue the relationship, as my graduation date was approaching. My close friends had seen the toxicity of my relationship, and they finally gave me an ultimatum: choose my daughter and friends or choose the relationship with my prick of a boyfriend. Many wonder why it's so hard to leave a toxic relationship, especially when children are involved. I grew up in a home with a lot of conflict and had witnessed a turbulent relation-ship between my parents. I thought it was normal and everyone went through it. Right? What I learned from my close friends is that it's not okay, this type of relationship was not normal, and it should not be tolerated. I remember feeling like a failure even though I knew my reasons for walking away justified my actions. And it felt different this time; walking away felt like the best decision for both of us.

Sometimes We Brew Some Kombucha

Newly single again, I realized I had spent enough time being distracted by the wrong things and not enough time being focused on what mattered most. It was time for me to refocus, throw myself into motherhood and school, and invest in my short- and long-term goals. Before I knew it, our lives started to shift, and it was like a ripple effect—something that happened when I chose to own my power. I had the power to control my attitude and to be brave and step forward out of the fog I had been in. It was miraculous. My energy shifted, and without much of an effort, my life was beginning to make sense. I had been focused on too many things: motherhood, school, work, social life, volunteering, and dating. I was so focused on the end goal, a better life for my daughter and a career, that I was going a hundred miles an hour just to get done what I needed to on any given day. I relied heavily on my family, friends, and even the system to do what I needed to in order to participate in my life. My family helped with laundry and with childcare in the evenings and on weekends when I was working, studying, or needing a night out. I was still young, and I needed to make the most of it. I woke up at 5:30 a.m. on most days to have time to prepare my schoolwork and get ready for the day before my daughter woke up. Fast-forward a few hours and she would be up and my routine with her started. Before we knew it, we were out the door and off to another day, racing to daycare and to school. The days were long. Sometimes, I didn't even pick up Hailey until 10:30 on the nights I had evening classes (that were required for graduation).

The driving force that pushes me forward has always been within me. But it wasn't until the loss of the relationships with the men I dated that I harnessed my power to live for myself and my daughter. My inner strength taught me that I was worth it, that I could do anything, and that I could accomplish any goal I set for us. Later, this strength of self translated to focusing on my health and well-being. I had gained more than sixty pounds during my pregnancy and after, and being single in the first few years of Hailey's life, I had been focused on her well-being and getting myself through school and work. As my self-esteem grew, the more I came to understand that I also needed to care for myself through exercise, nutrition, and self-care. I signed on at a local gym, registered for personal training sessions and nutrition coaching, and invested in myself. Though it was expensive (I worked a few extra shifts at Domino's Pizza to pay for the daycare at the gym), it soon became a part of our routine. I'll never forget walking through the gym after my workout and being stopped by someone who complimented me on how great I looked. To this day, I remember feeling proud; my hard work was paying off. Not only was I making a lifestyle change for myself but I was also setting a good example for my daughter. Over the course of two years, I lost more than thirty pounds, found a passion for nutrition, and learned how to live a healthy lifestyle.

It was during this timeframe that I had the urge to book my first trip to Varadero, Cuba, with my girlfriend. It was a brand-new experience; it was an opportunity to get out of my comfort zone. I loved meeting new people, experiencing new things, and enjoying the personal growth I found while on my travels. I became curious about exploring the world to see what it had to offer. When I returned home from my trip to Cuba, I had an opportunity to do some soul searching and realized I wanted more for my daughter and me than just any job or apartment. I knew I was gritty and resilient enough to make it happen. My daughter was thriving, our relationship was strong, and she was easy and happy. I realized how lucky I was to have such a strong and resilient baby girl.

My graduation was approaching, and I had begun searching for a job. In my final months of school, I spent hours sprucing up my cover letter and résumé and applying to any job that was in my field. I landed an interview at a local community health center. They were looking for a counselor, and I thought my degree was close enough to the job description, so I applied and got the job. After a few short months in the role, I realized I loved working in the field of mental health. I finally had enough money to move out of my parents' home, and I secured my first apartment with a roommate, although this arrangement was a short-lived one. I realized how heavily I had relied on family and friends to support my daughter and me, and living out on our own was very different.

I continued to focus on being grateful for what we had, and my life continued to evolve—good things kept coming my way. Just when I thought I would be single for eternity, as fate would have it, I met a guy, and not just any guy, but the one who would show me what true love, unconditional support, and partnership meant in a relationship. I wanted to do things differently this time. I wanted to be certain that he would stick around and could accept me and my daughter as a package. He asked me on a date, and I had arranged childcare, but the sitter was late. The world said it was meant to be: Before we even went on our first date, this man met my daughter. He smiled and spoke softly to her, and we patiently waited together for her babysitter to arrive. I immediately knew he was different, but I didn't want to get my hopes up, so I considered it a fluke. The date was great. It was full of laughter, good conversation, and a genuine interest in one another. The rest is history. When you know, you just know, and just like that, after two months of dating and my daughter's fourth birthday party (that he happily participated in), we moved into his new home. We accepted each other for who we were. We saw each other's drive, passion in our careers, and the desire to provide the best life we could for my daughter. We have been married for more than two years now and have been together for eight. The three of us make a family, along with our dogs, Duke, Diego, and Leonard.

By December, we celebrated our first Christmas, and we were in a groove with our ever-growing busy schedules. To ensure we had dedicated time together each week, we decided to coach Hailey's soccer team. We both loved being able to show her love and support while also giving back to the community. For my own growth, I applied to go back to school once again, this time for a bachelor's degree in social work at the University of Waterloo. I found mentors along the way who helped guide me to select the best professional development, challenged me to grow through self-reflection, and inspired me to continue my pursuit. Though it wasn't easy, in three years I graduated with my second undergraduate degree and was a social worker. Despite being proud of my accomplishments, I still felt there was more I could do for myself, my daughter, and my partner. So, I applied to the one-year program for a master's degree in social work (MSW) at Wilfrid Laurier University. I was accepted after a few months, and before I knew it, I was pursuing my MSW and working full time at the health center. I can never emphasize this enough: My journey would have looked a lot different without the love, gratitude, and support of my family and friends. So, lean into your support system and do what works for you.

And Sometimes We Sip on Lemon Margaritas

That's right, we are in Margaritaville now. Much of my journey in motherhood had been about survival, perseverance, and making it. What I didn't realize was just how much I would unravel in the process. It was an unlearning and unbecoming of all that wasn't true to my essence, so I could become who I was meant to be in the first place. I was meant to be a mother (something that hadn't dawned on me until this moment). But I was. Being a mother allowed my grit and resilience to blossom. It's what drove me to attend school full time, work long hours, and make something of myself. Before I found out I was pregnant, I was working as a pizza delivery driver, I had no life goals, and I had no ambitions to pursue anything more. Motherhood changed everything for me. I believe I'm exactly where I'm meant to be because of my unplanned pregnancy. I shifted toward gratitude, a growth mindset, and self-love. I owned and lived my truth of my commitment to better our lives through education, a career, health, nutrition, and fitness, and the knowledge and experience I've gained with my three degrees has helped shape me. These experiences have all empowered me to be the best mother, best partner, and best person for myself and my community. My partner, who witnessed the blossoming within me, encouraged me to take my dreams one step further by starting a business. The year 2017 was a big one for me: It was the year I began my work at Wilfrid Laurier University and the year I opened the doors to my private practice, Mindful Path Counselling.

Earlier this year I toyed around with the idea of returning to school (I swear for the last time!) to pursue a doctorate in educational leadership.

Without batting an eye, my husband and daughter were both on board with my pursuit for more. Knowing I had their support meant everything to me, so I applied and got in, yet both acceptance and doubt tugged at my heartstrings again. Old and unhealthy thought patterns plagued me, except this time, I was stronger than they were. I had the tools and resources to beat them and thrive. Now in my eighth course, I'm learning about leadership, vulnerability, emotional intelligence, and how to further develop my growth mindset. It's the unbridled feelings of positive esteem and knowing that this is the last step in my educational career to have the tools to reach my career potential. Some might ask why I continue to work two jobs, pursue further education, and throw myself into more personal growth and development. What on earth am I thinking? I know, I know . . . I'm doing that thing again where I go at the speed of light to see what I can accomplish.

Over the years I've come to embrace the chaos that is my life. I find that the less I resist it, the more everything flows together, even when it "shouldn't" make any sense. This pace fuels me for more, drives my ambitions, and keeps me excited about life, and I can happily share that I've cultivated a good balance between my role as a mother, partner, counselor, and small-business owner. My husband and I are pleased and content with our pursuits, our daughter is happy, and our life works for us. I will be a "forever student," and I think it's important to view life with that lens. There's much to learn about ourselves and others, what we can handle, what we are capable of, and the miracles that are possible. Each experience helps you veer out of your comfort zone and into the discomfort of the unknown, thus helping you understand that happiness comes from following your heart; a heart that is driven and guided by the passion and wisdom you develop in your journey to grow into being the best version of yourself.

chapter 18

JOURNEY TO HAPPINESS— LIVING YOUR TRUTH

JULIE CASS

"I hold the key
to my own
happiness..."

IG: @THEPOSITIVECHANGEGROUP
FB: @THEPOSITIVECHANGEGROUP
WWW.THEPOSITIVECHANGE.CA

JULIE CASS

Julie Cass is a transformational life and business coach and founder of The Positive Change Group. She has coached hundreds of business owners, leaders, and individuals over the years to help them tap into their full potential and create success. Julie is a CEO, a wife, and a mom. Her passion lies in helping busy people thrive in all facets of life by investing in the relationship they have with themselves.

Life is a journey of experiences, and for mo, tho richost moments in my life have always been centered around love. I am so grateful for my squad. Thank you to my partner and husband, Rob, who always reminds me that he is on my team. Izzy, Noah, Jamison, Courtney, and Taylor: I love you not only as our kids but as human beings. You inspire me to be a better person every day, and I am reminded by the blessings of you that having the courage to choose love and be true to myself is what brought you all in my life. Mom and Dad, I will always be grateful to the opportunities you provided me and the lessons I have learned from you. Love is the greatest healing gift of all.

> *"Have enough courage to trust love one more*
> *time and always one more time."*
>
> -Maya Angelou

The seeds of adventure and discovery . . .

Do you ever find yourself asking the questions, *Is this it? Is there more to life than this?*

There I was, twenty-four years old, lying in bed next to my husband with the following thoughts replaying themselves over and over again in my mind: *Is this happiness to you? Are you going to live like this for the rest of your life? Is there no more depth to this well we call life?*

To anyone from the outside looking in, it appeared that I had the picture-perfect life. I had a great husband, I was kicking ass in my career, and I had a fantastic family, home, and group of friends. You name it, I had it. I felt invincible.

So why did I continue to have this nagging feeling that wouldn't go away?

Why did I always fear that something bad was going to happen?

And why did I feel so guilty for thinking this way? I *should* be happy, right?

Asking myself these questions became the pivotal moment when my journey went deeper than what was visible to the naked eye. It was time to discover who I truly was beneath the accolades, the titles, and the picturesque life. It was time to lean into what I really desired. I realized that up until this point I was living by the ideals and beliefs of others. Yes, I came across as a strong and independent woman, but really, all I was doing was living on cruise control and not living my life at my pace, with my desires. And in my attempt to make others happy and do what was expected, I turned down the volume on my inner voice, my gut, my intuition. The irony is that when you suppress your voice, your expression, and your desires over and over again, at some point they will no longer simmer. Instead, they will bubble over, and that rage, resentment, and unhappiness will overflow like an explosive volcano.

What do you do when you are living in a life you no longer want? How do you choose your desires, your joy, when you know it will hurt so many people around you if you are honest about your feelings? Do you continue to suck it up, hoping things will change? Do you bury the feelings and pretend they don't exist in order to create peace and harmony? Or do you follow your truth, even though you know it will be messy?

In hindsight, I realize that my awakening came to me in my midtwenties. To some, this timeframe may sound absurd because our twenties, according to society, is the time for chasing all the things, being who we need to be, being who we think we should be, and doing the things we think we should be doing. Our twenties are disguised as freedom, but really, they're just a whole lotta "shoulding" keeping us in line with society around us. As for me, I always had a thirst for more, and at twenty-four-years-old, being married already and with resounding questions that only seemed to get louder the more I pushed them away,

I knew I was meant for more. Some may call it an existential crisis, but I wanted to understand the point of life and the role I played in it.

My thirst for this answer led me to meet people who were on a spiritual path. I say "spiritual" with hesitation because the word can turn people away. I was raised Catholic, but the ideals and principles of the religion did not resonate with me. I loved the messages from the Bible but did not like how they were interpreted. In my twenties, I was introduced to one of my first personal development books, *The Four Agreements*, written by Don Miguel Ruiz. This book opened a well inside me that I realized I had kept buried for so long. It led me to becoming a ravenous reader on anything I could find that related to mysticism, spirituality, past lives, the soul's journey, our higher intelligence, and meditation. You name it, I read it. I felt like I was reading ideas that were kept secret from 95 percent of the world. These topics surely weren't talked about in my household growing up. I realized that I wanted to go deeper, so I became certified in Reiki and trained in teaching yoga.

The more I continued my personal growth and development, the further I grew from my husband. I realized that I had a choice. I could either continue my path of self-discovery and leave an unfulfilled, unhappy marriage, or I could once again try to keep the peace, avoid ruffling any feathers, and put the lid back on, all while suppressing my inner voice that had finally woken after all these years.

Well, for me, the latter was not an option. That was when I knew I had to make decisions that honored my truth and were in alignment for me. My mind was made up to leave the life I knew, to walk away from comfort and stability and enter the unknown. Holy shit, that was scarier and harder than I could ever have imagined.

I ended my marriage, moved into a very small apartment, and did a "life" cleanse. Material things meant nothing to me anymore. Love, truth, fulfillment, and purpose were all more important.

To say it lightly, my family was less than thrilled. In fact, they could not handle my choice. Family values and maintaining the family honor had been drilled into my being from the time I was born. As someone who grew up in a family whose parents were Italian immigrants, my doing anything that went against the family honor was viewed as immoral and selfish.

As difficult as this time was for everyone, I realize when I look back that we all have our own conditioning and belief systems we bring into our world as we grow older. Our upbringing heavily influences our thoughts, behaviors, and patterns, and it is often hard to let go of those patterns, especially when they have been hardwired into us subconsciously over generations. Often, after living through war times and immigrating to a new country, our ancestors didn't have "being happy" at the forefront of their emotional or mental well-being. They were living in survival mode—it was all about ensuring that your family was safe, that there was food on the table, and that everyone was together, which is why I have immense compassion and love for those closest to me who couldn't support my life choices.

I realize all the decisions I made brought me to where I am today, even on the darkest nights of the soul when I thought I wouldn't survive. And for all of this, I feel grateful.

Life is an accumulation of choices that bring us exactly to where we need to be. Sometimes, we need to experience the hard times so we can really evaluate what is important to us, or maybe a difficult situation is a wake-up call for something we need to reassess so we can get back into alignment. But it all requires us to tune into who we are at our core, to listen to our inner voice, and to trust that it will never steer us down the wrong path.

While the choice to end my first marriage was a disappointment to many, I have no regrets whatsoever. It taught me to let go of the many judgments I had of others and myself. You see, my belief used to be that you meet someone you love and you get married and live happily ever after. The mere thought of divorce would have never crossed my mind!

Releasing my old beliefs and judgments allowed me to stay open to the love that was meant for me. It allowed me to fall in love with a man who had three kids from a previous marriage. The old Julie would never have seen love in that scenario. The old Julie would never have been capable of loving this man because for her, love was love only when it came in the "socially acceptable" package. What this experience taught me is that love in its purest form knows no bounds. It transcends race, gender, and socioeconomic status. The only boundaries we put on love are those based on our own beliefs and limitations.

The path to unconditional love

My journey to love is a continuous process. The more I love myself, the more I open myself to love in my life. I always say to my clients that the most important relationship you have is the one with yourself. If you can learn to love yourself deeply every day and expand the love you have for yourself, then the love with others will expand as well. Self-love goes beyond having a spa day. Deep self-love is messy. It's raw. It's being honest with yourself as you continue to shed everything that no longer serves your highest good. It's quieting that negative chatter in your head and choosing to fuel it with kindness, compassion, grace, and encouragement. It's allowing yourself to let go of the lower energies and vibrations you tolerate so you can maintain the peace and status quo. It's allowing yourself to disrupt your life and trust that you will find your way through just fine.

In my journey to love, I have released yet another passenger that was along for the ride. You know, the one who never has anything fun or constructive to contribute but instead is constantly dragging you down? Yes, you guessed it . . . guilt. Letting go of guilt and the self-deprecation that often accompanied it felt freeing, like an invisible weight had lifted off me. I finally felt worthy of being loved and giving my love freely and openly as well. I realized that many of my choices earlier in life were guided from a space of guilt.

Releasing guilt allowed me to increase my threshold for joy instead of limiting myself from experiencing it. I used to think that "you can't experience too much good" or that "you have to wait for the other shoe to drop." These were familiar mantras to me. For a long time, living from a place of fear felt normal and living from a place of love and joy felt rebellious. These feelings created great stress in my life because they didn't represent my true self; they were emotions and beliefs I adopted/fabricated that became my reality.

Sometimes, these feelings still show up for me, but not as often now that I have my husband who loves me for me. He does not try to change me or squash any of my dreams. He has helped me experience unconditional love and has stood by me in my darkest moments with no judgment.

Where my blocks show up is in my capacity to receive this love. The guilt that I often entertained put a cap on how much love I could take in. I could easily sabotage moments that were beautiful because I couldn't contain that joy, or worse, I felt like it was too good to be true. Yikes.

Self-love is a commitment to continually assess where our blocks stem from so we can consciously work on releasing them. And yes, even though I am more aligned in my truth, my journey, and my evolution, there is still work to be done with my capacity to receive love in my life instead of limiting it. And *this* is something we each can control.

So, love yourself. Love yourself hard and love yourself true because that is something directly within your control and that you can cultivate day by day. You will attract those people in your life who will meet you where you are. And then, when you find your "partner," make a commitment to evolve yourself every day. My husband and I had unconventional marriage vows, and an unconventional wedding. I vowed, "I promise to work on myself every day, to evolve into the best version of me, and to do the work necessary for growth—to grow with you in our relationship." The biggest gift you can give to yourself and your partner is to allow them the space to do their inner work, to trust that they are doing so, and to embrace their evolution in the process. Allow yourself to come into your season of becoming, whatever that looks and feels like for you.

Deepening self-love through motherhood

One of the greatest gifts in my life is my children. I am blessed to have two children and three stepchildren. Having a blended family has not always been easy, but I would not trade it for the world. Motherhood has been my greatest and deepest self-love journey yet. When I first became a mom, I realized that there is no other role you could play in your life as selfless as this one. I will do anything for my kids. And I mean anything! The love I feel for my kids is like no other. Call it divine, one-of-a-kind, or higher-intelligence love—it is limitless and unconditional.

I have learned over the years that the best gift of love I can give to my kids is this: Teach them to listen to their inner voice. Help them turn up the volume on their inner truth and let that be their true guardian angel in this life, especially in a time when there is so much external influence and distraction through social media and more.

I believe that modern-day warfare isn't fought with bombs and guns, it's the battle that takes place daily in our heads. It's the destructive and self deprecating voices that we give way too much energy to. Too often, I find myself falling into the trap of wanting to *tell* my kids what to do because I am their mom and I know best. But I catch myself just in time because the truth is, there's a fine line between wanting the best for someone and knowing what's best for them. I don't always know what's best. My idea will always be tinged with my own filters and preconceived notions based on my own life experiences. What I can do instead is be an example. I can *show* them what it feels like and looks like to share my truth, to live my truth, to follow my inner moral compass, and to pursue joy, love, and abundance in every way.

To that same degree, I also believe that we have much to learn from our kids. I have come to see my kids as divine, wise beings who need to tap into their truth sooner rather than later. Imagine the liberation we would all feel if we could learn to live our truths from a young age. The pursuit to happiness would be far less bumpy. Life would still have its challenges, but they wouldn't be as devastating or severe since you know how to self-regulate emotionally, mentally, and physically to navigate the bumps you encounter on your journey. When you are living in alignment with your truth, you no longer need to step out of it or have harsh awakenings to know what does or does not resonate for you any longer.

My lifelong itinerary for joy

All these experiences I've shared with you have one theme in common: a commitment to self-accountability and self-love—a radical, deep, messy self-love. You are responsible for your own happiness. If everyone lived by this principle, the world would be a better place. You are not responsible for making anyone happy but yourself. Doesn't that take a load off of you? Roll your shoulders, unclench that jaw, and take a deep breath and release. You are in the driver's seat of your own life.

To that same effect, if we are responsible for our own happiness, then we are also responsible for our own misery. We are responsible for our state of mind, the life we create, and how we choose to live it. This truth was the most empowering one I learned. Every day I remind myself that I hold the key to my happiness, that I make choices that can either create harmony or upset, and that when I take care of myself, my family is better for it.

I am passionate about empowering women to find the courage to find, share, and live their truth, to be in control of their lives and work on their subconscious minds to upgrade their beliefs and identity so they can be in alignment with their highest and best selves.

I believe one reason that we have so much heartache, depression, and anxiety is because we have become a go-go-go society. We distract ourselves from our true essence and our true power, which is why we use our surrounding environment for validation and direction in almost every aspect of our lives. The only way you can discover your life path and true essence is by quieting the noise around you— the inner mean girl, the voices of others in your head, the expectations you place on yourself, and the expectations you take on. Hush. Go deep within your soul and you'll find the answers you're looking for.

Today, at forty-five years wise, I finally find myself fulfilled and living my truth. I am at peace with myself and no longer at war within. It doesn't mean my life is perfect or without bumps and curveballs; instead, what I know to be true every step of the way is this:

By pure osmosis, happiness elevates others.

We become less reactive and argumentative when living in alignment with our truth. Wanna test it out? Observe yourself the next time you're triggered. You become a magnet for love. And I believe this is our human currency and our deepest truth. Love beyond what you can even imagine.

We are multidimensional beings, and it is about time we live our lives with this truth in mind. Finding self-love and self-empowerment is a holistic journey filled with seasons, peaks, and valleys. Don't settle for parts of the journey—ask for it all! You deserve everything that you desire; you are worthy of it. If, as you read this chapter, you're wondering, *Who am I to have it all?*

Who are you not to? Why not you?

These are the questions I asked myself and still do every day. I remind myself each day that I am worthy to receive, I am worthy to be happy, I am worthy to align my career with my purpose, and I am worthy of success and deep love. And so are you!

closing note

FOREVER BECOMING. EVER BLOOMING.

TANIA JANE MORAES–VAZ

"We are the divine portal. The creatrix. The phoenix. The seer. The goddess. The warrioress. The wise woman. The maiden. The mother. The crone. We have the wisdom of generations past within us. It's time to harness that power."

TANIA JANE MORAES—VAZ

Tania Jane Moraes-Vaz is a woman with many capes: wife and mama, self-expression mentor and storyteller, energetic light-worker, overall creative strategist, five-time best-selling author, host of *The Holistic Warrior Life* podcast, and brand photographer. She is the founder of The Holistic Warrior Life Co. and Warrior Life Creative Co.—a full-scale creative agency specializing in nurture content marketing for heart-inspired entrepreneurs and brands. She is also a creative partner / developmental editor with the YGTMamaMedia Co. and *Mama Brain Magazine*.

After losing her way for three years working in corporate hedge funds, fintech, and marketing, she is finally putting her BA in English Literature and Creative Writing from the University of Waterloo to some excellent use. Like Alice who ventured down the rabbit hole, Tania found her way back to her soul-calling of storytelling and self-expression through a series of "yes"-ventures in the world of writing, publishing, and entrepreneurship.

Tania has worked with top six-figure business owners and small business brands to create compelling copy and content that converts and engages. She has mentored more than 120 authors, has helped grow a start-up from sixteen authors to more than a hundred within two years, has hosted a sold-out live event, has been featured on the radio and more than a dozen podcasts, and she is just getting started.

To all women, there's a warrioress within you dying to unleash herself and her magic. Lean in. Always.

I raise up my voice—not so that I can shout, but
so that those without a voice can be heard....
We cannot all succeed when half of us are held
back.

~ Malala Yousafzai

And there from the depths of the ashes,

She continued to rise up.

Shoulders back, chin up.

A fiery sight to see.

Marred with ashes of triumph and loss.

Crown of flower and thorns gracing her head.

She had seen it all within this lifetime.

Quite certain she had lived a thousand lifetimes within her
present one.

Loss. Betrayal. Love. Birth. Success. Desire. And more.

And as she continued to climb through the mountains that
were only hers to scale,

she realized she moved with a flow that was innately hers.

A flow filled with effortless grace and grit.
She realized that she no longer shied away from discomfort;
she embraced it.
She no longer suppressed her truth, her expression, her
desires; she claimed them.
She no longer settled for "it's fine" or "it's okay." She stood in
her strength, her inner
knowing, her truth, and owned it. Unapologetically.

Yes, she had come full circle.
From damsel in distress to finally standing tall and asking,
"Why not me?"
She created her own tables where all were welcome—truth,
discomfort, pain,
generational trauma and healing, shadow work, and
unapologetic conversations.
She reclaimed herSELF boldly, without second-guessing her
next moves.
She had finally come home to herself, skin and bones, heart
and soul.

No longer were there a thousand miles that separated her
from her true essence.
Instead, one foot in front of the other, she continued her
climb, her ascend to herself.
Befriending luscious fruit—some sweet like honey, some
lemony tart.
These were the fruits of her labor, fruits that provided her
sustenance on her path to

becoming who she always was.

Who she was always meant to be.

She is you. And she is me.

Together we climb our mountains, though different in altitude and terrain, our voices and

truths forever echoing and resounding in the spaciousness that is our heart.

You are safe now. Lay down your armor. You are home now, Warrioress.

* * *

There you have it: Life, Love, Lemonade—an ode to the woman we were, the woman we are, and the woman we are always becoming. As I write these words, I'd love to say that one year has passed and things look different. They don't. We are still playing the "open today, locked down tomorrow" lottery ticket, hoping for the best . . . for our children, for us, for our loved ones, for our businesses. And yet, at the same time, so much has changed. Evolved. We have evolved. We have adapted as we always do. Our strength has been repeatedly tested. Our loyalties have been questioned in the wake of global upheaval on home turf and overseas. Our sanity is on the brink of collapsing more days than none as we navigate every single emotion in the book while still juggling womanhood, motherhood, #ceobabe, #workingmom, #pinterestmom, and all other hashtags.

The themes in this book have all centered around a longing for self, bold expression, love, and respect. And every chapter reaffirms that we must be that which we desire. That within us lies the power to raise ourselves up, to build up our courage, and to live our life with confidence and conviction. And if there is anything I am more certain of as I reflect over every single woman's story within this book, it's this one thing: Women are natural-born leaders. Think like massive empress energy, babe.

And as women, we have it in us to weather every storm that comes our way, find the sliver of sunshine that slowly shines through, making the most of the wreckage that lies in front of us. We are the divine portal. The creatrix. The phoenix. The seer. The goddess. The warrioress. The wise woman. The maiden. The mother. The crone. We have the wisdom of generations past within us. It's time to harness that power. It is time to lean into massive self- trust. It's time to trust our intuition and honor our voices. It's time to take up space freely and unapologetically. It's time to lean into massive self-love, mothering ourselves every step of the way. Much like how lemons, though tart and tangy, have their purpose, so, too, are our experiences, past and present. We wouldn't be who we are without them. And we certainly wouldn't know what we are capable of.

And so, I want you to ask yourself these questions (feel free to journal or reflect in your own way):

- At what point did love mean submerging your desires and needs deep within yourself?
- At what point did you stop listening to the call of your heart?
- At what point did you stop truly glowing and radiating the pulsating energy of who you are as a woman?
- At what point did you subdue your sensuality, your essence, your ferocity, your desires?

- What was it that you desired as a child? As a young woman? As a woman who has multiple universes buried within her?
- What is it that you desire within your relationships, partnerships, friendships?
- Have you given that to yourself?
- Have you been that to yourself?
- At what point did you think that being enough, being a woman meant stepping on and squashing your own dreams, wants, and desires so that you could settle for what looks "good" or "perfect" or "enough" for others?
- At what point did you start settling for what checked off the boxes on paper? For what looked picture perfect, just how society demands it to be?
- At what point did you stop being who you are and who you needed to be for yourself so you could be who/what they wanted you to be?
- How old were you when you first dimmed your light? Your self-expression?
- When was the first time you stopped shining brightly as your unique self and aimed to blend in with everyone else? Why?

Sit with these questions and honor the emotions, truths, and somatic sensations that surface. Be gentle with yourself. Honor your path, your journey, your wins, and your losses (though even those have wins hidden within them). Every single day, reparent yourself and love on yourself with the same grace and love you would your own child or best friend. If this is the first time you are tapping into the depths of your life's journey, know that healing is never linear. It surfaces in parts, spaces, and kaleidoscopic lenses. You are here now. You have a sisterhood within every single woman in this book. Reach out. Connect. Move toward the energetic pulls you desire.

May every single story in this book be proof that anything is possible. That even when you think all is lost, therein lies your best possibility to expand and evolve into more of who you're destined and designed to be. Throughout this book, these truths reverberate loud and clear. May these be your anthem whenever you need to remind yourself of who you truly are:

I am powerful and worthy beyond measure.
I am uniquely designed and created with purpose and intention.
My voice matters.
I matter.
I am worthy of love and respect. From myself and others.
I will no longer dim my light, suppress my voice, and hide my truth to keep others comfortable or safe. Including myself.
I will forever lean into expansion, with all its curves and edges.
I will continue to come home to myself, one breath and one step at a time.

And so, I pray for you and unto you that you will
Be a moving prayer of that very intention.
That, my sweet soul, is an embodiment of your deepest desires.

Release the ties that keep you bound to stagnancy, limitations, and others' projections.
Create an intention for yourself, your life, your business.
Look for the drops of lemonade and create your own elixir that fuels you and nourishes you—mind, body, and soul.

You have to go first; you have to lead the way.
All else will align and fall into place.

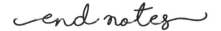

CHAPTER 1 BY ANDREA MOURAD

Opening quote: https://www.goodreads.com/quotes/60389-even-after-all-this-time-the-sun-never-says-to, retrieved March 28, 2021.

CHAPTER 2 BY ANDREA SLUGA

Opening quote: https://www.goodreads.com/quotes/627413-it-is-far-better-to-be-exhausted-from-success-than, retrieved March 28, 2021.

CHAPTER 3 BY ANITA VOLIKIS

Opening quote: Oliver, Mary. *House of Light*. 1st ed. Beacon Press, 1992.

1. Singer, M. A. *The Untethered Soul: The Journey Beyond Yourself*. Oakland, CA: Noetic Books, Institute of Noetic Sciences, New Harbinger Publications, 2007.

CHAPTER 4 BY ERIN MONTGOMERY

Opening quote: Austen, Jane. *Pride and Prejudice*. New York: Knopf, 1991.

CHAPTER 5 BY TRACY LYNNE KEEPING

Opening quote: Geurs, Karl, dir. *Pooh's Grand Adventure: The Search for Christopher Robin.* Disney, 1997.

CHAPTER 6 BY MICHELLE NICOLET

Opening quote: https://www.goodreads.com/quotes/7532767-forgive-yourself-for-not-knowing-what-you-didn-t-know-before, retrieved March 28, 2021.
1. https://www.lexico.com/en/definition/wake-up_call, retrieved March 28, 2021.
2. Fournier, Denise PhD. Psychology Today. "The Only Way to Eat an Elephant." Blog. April 24, 2018. https://www.psychologytoday.com/us/blog/mindfully-present-fully-alive/201804/the-only-way-eat-elephant, retrieved on March 28, 2021.

CHAPTER 7 BY JENNIFER O'HARE

Opening quote: Brown, Hannah. The Remote Yogi. "25 Inspiring Quotes to Break Free from People Pleasing." Blog. March 5, 2021. https://theremoteyogi.blog/2021/03/05/quotes-for-people-pleasing/, retrieved March 29, 2021.

CHAPTER 8 BY KIRSTI STUBBS COLEMAN

Opening quote: Doyle, Glennon. *Untamed.* New York: The Dial Press, 2020.

CHAPTER 9 BY KAT INOKAI

Opening quote: Carroll, Lewis. *Alice's Adventures in Wonderland.* SDE Classics, 2019.

CHAPTER 10 BY TONI RONAYNE

Opening quote: https://www.goodreads.com/quotes/54375-love-is-the-strongest-force-the-world-possesses-and-yet, retrieved March 28, 2021.

CHAPTER 11 BY MICHELLE TONN

Opening quote: Rumi Quotes. BrainyQuote.com, BrainyMedia Inc, 2021. https://www.brainyquote.com/quotes/rumi_597890, accessed April 5, 2021.

CHAPTER 12 BY MELISSA PUNAMBOLAM

Opening quote: http://www.guyana.org/proverbs.html, retrieved March 31, 2021.

CHAPTER 13 BY GINA BRIGANDI

Opening quote: https://themindsjournal.com/sometimes-in-life-your-situation/, retrieved March 28, 2021.

CHAPTER 14 BY CASIE SCORIE

Opening quote: https://www.awakenthegreatnesswithin.com/35-inspirational-quotes-on-following-your-heart/, retrieved March 28, 2021.

CHAPTER 15 BY NATHALIE AMLANI

Opening quote: Hay, Louise and Robert Holden. *Life Loves You: 7 Spiritual Practices to Heal Your Life.* Hay House Inc., 2016.
1. Sincero, Jen. *Badass Habits.* Viking, 2020.

CHAPTER 16 BY CHIARA FRITZLER

Opening quote: https://www.goodreads.com/quotes/15244-there-were-always-in-me-two-women-at-least-one, retrieved March 28, 2021.

CHAPTER 17 BY STEPHANIE DINSMORE

Opening quote: Brown, Brené. *The Gifts of Imperfection: Let Go of Who You Think You're Supposed to Be and Embrace Who You Are.* Center City, Minnesota: Hazelden, 2010.

CHAPTER 18 BY JULIE CASS

Opening quote: Hogan, Brianne. The Date Mix. "25 Trust Quotes from Relationships That Can Bring You Closer." Blog. May 11, 2020. https://www.zoosk.com/date-mix/quotes/trust-quotes-for-relationships/, retrieved March 29, 2021.

CLOSING NOTE BY TANIA JANE MORAES—VAZ

Opening quote: https://malala.org/newsroom/archive/malala-un-speech, retrieved April 10, 2021.

YGTMedia Co. is a blended boutique publishing house for mission-driven humans. We help seasoned and emerging authors "birth their brain babies" through a supportive and collaborative approach. Specializing in narrative nonfiction and adult and children's empowerment books, we believe that words can change the world, and we intend to do so one book at a time.

www.ygtmama.com/publishing

@ygtmama.media.co

@ygtmama.media.co

Made in the USA
Monee, IL
09 May 2021

67865261R00154